Da Black Book of Linguistic Liberation

C. Liegh McInnis

Psychedelic Literature/Jackson, Mississippi

Psychedelic Literature ®

203 Lynn Lane
Clinton, MS 39056
(601) 383-0024
psychedeliclit@bellsouth.net

LCCN: 2001 132073
ISBN: (13 digit) 978-0-9655775-6-4
ISBN: (10 digit) 0-9655775-6-2

Other Works by C. Liegh McInnis

Matters of Reality: Body, Mind & Soul (Poetry, 1997)
The Lyrics of Prince (Lyrical Criticism, 1997, 2001)
Scripts: Sketches and Tales of Urban MS (Fiction, 1998)
Confessions: Brainstormin' from Midnight 'til Dawn (Poetry, 1998)
Searchin' 4 Psychedelica (Poetry, 1999)
Prose: Essays and Letters (Social Commentary, 1999)
Poetic Discussions (Interviews, DVD 2005)
Introduction of a Blues Poet (Poetry, CD 2005)

Acknowledgments

To God: Thank you for allowing me to become better than [i] was yesterday.

To Monica Taylor-McInnis...for who we used to be, who we are, and where we are headed. Every step with you has been an excursion in spiritual ecstasy. Heaven is where you are.

For Family and Friends...Foundation is what we all need. Thank you for letting me build my crib on y'all.

For the people in West Jackson...Black folk be living. Paint today any color you want—it's all black on the inside.

For JSU...Home is where the heart is, and my heart is there.

For the griots before and the griots to come...clothe me in your righteousness; lend me your eyes and guide my tongue.

To Ahmos and Ywemboui, Jolivette, David, Derrick, Doc Ward, Doc Martin, Kalamu, Charlie, Nayo, Doc OBJ, Uganda, Ramona, Judy, M.U.G.A.B.E.E., Ezra, Preselfannie, Mattie, Tony, Nikki B., and Howard: Thanks for letting me be y'alls sponge. Keep raining on me.

For Black people everywhere: Let's learn to love ourselves as much as we love everyone else.

For you: Thank you for making my work a part of your life. [i] hope it adds something that u can use. Peace, rain, and sunshine...rainbows forever.

Epigraph

"I yam what I am!" Ellison has his hero say exuberantly, the act of punning, a form of *linguistic liberation*, expressing and corresponding to his psychological liberation"

Walter B. Rideout—"Foreword," *The Militant Black Writer in Africa and America*

"Taking the white man's language, dislocating his syntax, recharging his words with new strength and sometimes with new meaning before hurling them back in his teeth, while upsetting his self-righteous complacency and clichés, our poets rehabilitate such terms as Africa and blackness, beauty and peace."

Mercer Cook—*The Militant Black Writer in Africa and America*

"Black writers are 'militant' only to white and black people who think white. To say "I'm black" in America is an act of resistance. To say out loud, 'I'm black, and I'm proud,' is an act of rebellion; to attempt systematically to move black people to act out of their beauty and their blackness in white America is to foment revolution. To write black poetry is an act of survival, of regeneration, of love...[Black writers] write for black people and they write about their blackness, and out of their blackness, rejecting anyone and anything that stands in the way of self-knowledge and self-celebration"

Stephen Henderson—*The Militant Black Writer in Africa and America*

"Open up, Black writers. Open up. Blow. Yeah, blow those white dreams and demons away. Kill the beast of a fetid literary tradition. Blow them away. Open up. Link up with the struggle. Confront yourselves. Do your thing whenever and wherever you can. Talk to each other. Your own magazines and journals. Your own films and playhouses. Your own critique. White writers can teach you very little. Perhaps some precise kind of technique. But Stevie Wonder's technique is finally hipper than T. S. Eliot's. Talk to each other. No alienation in white liberal zones. Embrace Black people; experiment with Black styles. What, for example, is the meaning of the boogaloo? I mean it. James Brown is the best poet we got baby."

Larry Neal—*Negro Digest*. January, 1968. Quoted in *The Militant Black Writer in Africa and America*.

Table of Contents

Black Man   7
Mississippi Courage: A Lighthouse to the World   10
What Good Are Poems?   12
It's Libation Time   13
Griot Space   15
A Poem for Lorenzo Thomas' Post-Modern
       Concerns   16
Don't Call Me Angry   17
For Maryemma G.   19
Blue Colored Glasses (for Pecola)   20
[i] Can't Dance (The Middle-Class
       Afro-American Blues Song)   21
Poetry Is...   23
Appreciation of You (in three Parts)   24
The Sweetness of Life (for Walter Payton)   26
Bob Moses: Gardener of Minds   29
What You Can Say in a Poem...?   30
Movements in Blackness: Shades of Humanity   33
Impotence   35
Equal Tears   36
[i] Know It Was the Blood   37
Tree of Life (Black Colleges Be Here)   39
Oral Surgery   42
Put the Ghosts to Rest (for Rainey Pool)   43
A Poem for Bennie, Byrd, and the Black Caucus 45
Chivalry, Sexism, or Revolution?   47
Music Is   48
Census Blues   52
Revelations of a Bastard Child   53
For Hollis and His Southern Echo   56
Religion Haiku   58
The Preamble to the Homeless Constitution   59
How Do [i] Describe?   61
Mississippi's Millennium Education   62
Redistricting Blues   64
Get Yo' Child a Library Card   65
Much to Do about Marginalization   67

Do We Believe in Nature?   68
The Poison of Integration   69
Truth Haiku   70
No Revolution Today   71
2G (Another Millennium Poem)   72
The Cruelest Thing (for Kysha N. Brown)   73
My People   74
Sex Poem   75
[i]'m Sick of Blues Poets   76
Ms. Betty: A Silent Warrior   78
To Charlie   79
Don't Pick the Fruit too Soon   80
A Ghetto Sunday   81
We Be Ground Gods   82
Temptation in Haiku Movements   83
For Imperfect People (Joe Starks' Lament)   84
Come Home   85
This Is not a Protest Poem   86
Writing Alone at Night (for Li Po and Tu Fu)   90
What's My Name?   91
Whatever "It" Is that We Want   95
The Apology: Blood on the Typewriter   96

"[i]'m testing positive for the funk.
[i]'d gladly pee in anybody's cup.
And if your cup overflows,
[i]'m testing positive and pee somemo'."
from "We Can Funk"

Prince and George Clinton

Black Man

[i] apologize for marching my muddy waters feet
on your pasty pat boone carpet, but my steps have been
made dusty from dancing in the dirt of the Delta.
So, allow me to straighten your crooked records.
[i] am history. My name is Black,
but you can call me "Daddy Pop"
'cause [i]'m father to the rainbow.
[i] got more child-nations than Skittles got colors
all birthed from the rich womb of Alkebu-lan.
Even my outhouse produces flowering countries.
My loins are the kaleidoscope of life.
[i] am the prism the creates the spectrum of humanity.
My bountiful body is as fertile as the Nile reservoir,
and my soul shines like the son's Aton.
[i] was a Muslim before you submitted,
Christ-like before the crucifixion,
and a mason before the codes.
[i] created remedial education for Socrates.
[i] was the one who suggested the elephant to Hannibal,
the donkey to Yeshua, and the Cadillac to Reverend Ike.
[i] was the one who taught Merlin
that damn sleight of hand trick;
still you call me witch doctor and call him wizard;
as the government works its hoo doo,
hell, [i] need some voo doo jus' to stay sane.
If you don't think that [i]'m a magician
jus' check me out on bill day.
How does fourteen percent of the population
give a whole nation so much soul?

7

If the one drop rule applies,
then the complete commonwealth gots to be colored.
[i] was the one who did the driving and parallel parking
long before Columbus double parked in a red zone.
[i] tried to warn my carmine brothers
'bout smoking that pipe with Captain Smith.
[i]'m Nat Turner on my best day
and Clarence Thomas on my worst,
but even my worst doesn't erase the supreme of my being.
[i]'m B. B. King on Saturday night
and Martin Luther King on Sunday morning.
[i]'m the beautiful fiery Truth of Richard Pryor and
the crackling communal Wisdom of Baba Gregory.
[i] am Frederick Douglass with a Kangol slightly tilted
to the side, still refusing to relinquish my plantation house.
[i]'m Booker T. Washington in a red, pinstriped
double-breasted suit with red silk socks
and a pair of shiny Stacey Adams.
[i]'m gon' pull myself up by my wingtips
and look good doing it.
[i]'m the double talking, double consciousness of Du Bois
and the glorious, steadfast rock of Garvey.
[i]'m the "New Negro"—of every ten years.
[i] made the peanut give birth to things that
you wouldn't believe, and [i] coordinated red, yellow, and
green to keep white folks from running into each other.
By the way—how you gon' invent a cotton gin
when you ain't picked no cotton?
If necessity is the mother of invention, then every
patent in America should be inscribed in my blood.
[i] tried to tell Custard not to go in betwixt them rocks.
[i] took on wings at Tuskegee
and taught America how to fly.
[i] pumped electrifying, orgasmic life
into your comatose language.
[i]'m the same man who cut Malcolm's conk
and gives Reverend Sharpton his touch-up.
[i] was the one who said, "Run, Jesse, run."
[i]'m Robert Johnson, Chuck Berry, Thelonious Monk,

Miles Davis, Little Richard, Jackie Wilson, James Brown,
Jimi Hendrix, Smokey Robinson, Stevie Wonder,
Marvin Gaye, and Tina Turner
all sprouting from the same root.
That's right. [i]'m ⚥ !
(The Artist Formerly Known as All that Has Come)
which makes me the sound of the universe
before the pale pirates took control.
But above all else, [i] am forever here
like a stain on the silk shirt of white supremacy.
[i] have survived more wars and famines than McDonald's
has sold over priced and over processed scamburgers.
[i] have survived more conspiracies than an
Oliver Stone movie and more cliffhangers than
Dynasty, *Falcon Crest*, *Dallas* and *General Hospital*.
That's why my *Young* are so damn *Restless*.
[i] am the bulging, pounding phallic anxiety of a nation.
You don't know whether to
emasculate me, incarcerate me, infect me, or ejaculate me.
That's alright 'cause [i] can't help but
swagger and swing as I slide down the street.
The music in my rhythm gives me more bounce to my beat.
[i] am JSU and Tougaloo, the public and private HBCU.
And one day [i]'m gon' use my education
to engineer my sovereignty.
Until then [i]'ll keep bumping my blues on the one.
Poverty and oppression are
jus' more opportunities to be great.
[i]'m too bad to die, too proud not to live
and too funky not to enjoy it all.
The only time that [i] give up my wooly-headed existence
is so that others may have everlasting life.

**"Mississippi Courage: A Lighthouse to the World
(for Medgar, Fannie Lou, and Ms. Annie Devine)"**

Courage is a lighthouse guiding ships to salvation.
Courage is a fire that burns down the dead weeds of racism
that rise to suffocate the voices of liberty.
Courage is an antibiotic that kills the bacteria of hatred.
Courage was the nucleus of the Mississippi Trinity.
Three lamps full of freedom oil that shined the path to the
dirt and gravel roads of liberation:
an insurance salesman, a sharecropper, and a teacher.
Three instructors of liberation, teaching that
righteous knees only bow before God and that
the children of God have an unyielding, organic duty
to protect the meek like umbrellas shielding us
from the acid showers of colonialism or overcoats
shielding us from the frozen winds of prejudice.
Three bucking broncos, railing against
pale cowboys who lurk in the dark of the night
armed with the silver bullets of white supremacy.
Three lambs of justice who boldly walked into
the snake pit of the South and the lion's den of America
to snatch their freedom from Ross "Nebuchadnezzar"
Barnett, Pharaoh Bilbo, and his side-winding,
salamandering scribes, the *Jackson Daily News*.
The insurance salesman, the sharecropper,
and the teacher bore the cross of change.
They were the fertile soil in which we planted our seeds of
hope, as they petitioned us to invest the collateral of our
talents into the mutual fund of the movement.
That's why we must be tired of paper-tiger intellectuals
and playboy revolutionaries who care more about their
Cadillac payments than tilling the soil of ebony education
as they are standing on the backs and trampling the fruits
of Medgar, Fannie Lou, and Ms. Annie Devine.
These three midwifed and nurtured the germination
of the movement, which caused a rippling of
flowers and trees sprouting through
the winter of racism into the spring of transformation.

Like Shaka they were the pounding tom-tom heart of a
militant movement, like Jesus they came to heal the sick,
and like Mohammed they laid the blueprint for their people.
Still everyday people fighting for everyday concerns.
Speaking volumes with their actions, this trinity shook
the fibers of the universe.
Through intellectual guerrilla warfare with the spirit of
Jomo Kenyatta, they showed that leaders can't teach people
to stand as tall as mighty magnolia trees if they are
weeping willows bowing on their knees to the winds of
wrongdoers; they embraced the sword of justice and the
fires of protest becoming ministers for justice and preachers
of the gospel of freedom, teaching us to be the engine of
organizations rather than be driven or plowed over by them.
With little possessions, they fought for the dispossessed,
each one crying 900,000 jubilee tears for 900,000 of
Wright and Walker's citizens at the mercy of mis-educated
teachers and chicken eating preachers, all the while
refusing to fight the forest fire of evil with evil, believing
love to be the only antidote for hate—for when held to the
light of Truth courage is the mirrored reflection of love,
and no greater love than a man who would lay down his
chivalric cashmere coat of life for another so that we may
walk unblemished over the cesspool of struggle—his
payment to be beaten, kicked, sprayed, spit on, spied on,
lied on, bombed, and tuned out by his own for a few
crumbs of token positions and jus' enough money to move
cross the tracks into the homes that pale people abandoned
to preserve the marmalade of Mississippi tradition.
In the blood-stained name of emancipation, equality, and
liberty the thick sweet potato aroma of their lingering
legacy demands that we heed the call to explode this
corrupt cocoon into a Capital city of concrete citizens.

So, [i] don't know if [i]'m going to heaven or hell,
but wherever [i]'m going, [i]'m going for Mississippi.
[i]'m going for Mississippi.

What Good Are Poems?

Can a poem be as effective as a .357?
Can the images of a poem spray buck shot holes
into the body of a greenback stuffed sheet wearing shoat?
Can a poem be thrown as a brick through the window
of a grocery store so that we may pillage and plunder
its shelves for food for the hungry?
Can a poem be laid on top of a poem,
be laid on top of a poem, be laid on top of a poem
until we have built a shelter for the homeless?
Does a poem need a million dollar war chest
or a foundation grant to be mightier than the sword?
What good does a poem do a spoiled, bloated belly?
Can a poem lay hands on the sick and clothed the naked?
Can a poem work hoodoo on an ACT score?
Can a poem pull the rent payment from a magician's hat?
Can poems assassinate Negro turncoats
who have sold their souls to racist rags?
Can poems cut short the lives of serpentine superintendents
who slyly suffocate African babies in Euro-excrement
disguised as Caucasian curriculums?

Poets are the African bees of political pollination.
Poems are the sperm of revolution.
We need poets to stop adding extra syrup and saccharin
to their sonnets so as to appease the pale palates of people
who have not the stomach for the straight-no-chaser truth.
We need poets to stop mindlessly
masturbating away their talents into literary napkins.
We need poets to start impregnating thoughts of
Black magnolias bursting through white cement
into the minds of Raven virgin souls who without it
toil in the reproductive process of self-aversion.

Poems are the sperms of revolution.
Are you making love to your people,
or are you merely fornicating away your existence?

It's Libation Time

It's libation time for the spirit soldiers of Christ whose
misty feet still leave footprints of a bloody map from this
middle passage while the wind of history blows sweet the
breath of God, which is the lingering sugary smell of
salvation for the South
earned on the backs of Onyx Angels.
Black people are the fertile soil
in which God planted his seeds for a holy nation
as we eat greens with our fingers
after building a nation with our hands,
growing strong from nature's bounty
the body of God springing forth from vines and trees.
How else could a people survive the peculiar institution?
God is the power to inhale, pulling into the nostrils
the honey-soaked, revitalizing breath of the lamb.
God is the strength to exhale,
releasing the toxins of unholy living,
cleansing the human vessel to be driven by the Holy Spirit.
How else does the family tree survive
the merciless termites of the middle passage?
How else does the family tree survive
the malicious maggots of miscegenation.
How else do you survive picking cotton
'til yo' hands become stained with concrete calluses,
'til yo' spine becomes a rickety, shattered step ladder,
and 'til yo' feet are swollen sandpaper?
God is better than Calamine Lotion for yo' hands.
God is better than Ben Gay for yo' back.
God is better than Dr. Scholl's for yo' feet.
God was the pure water of the slaves' noon-day drink
and the yams that fueled their weary bodies.
It's libation time because unlike Lincoln's dog and pony
contract of smoke and mirrors,
God's proclamation in an iron-clad treaty of
complete emancipation
'cause the ink of God's freedom document
is the blood of the lamb that no man can wash away

for God won't renege on his reconstruction
like federal troops withdrawing from the South
leaving our heads firmly in the jaws of
the State's Luciferioius lion-like legislation
because
God is the sweet potato soul of Negro Spirituals.
God is the cast-iron Truth
of Brown vs. the Board of Education.
God is the ferociously fanged Freedom
of the 13th Amendment.
God is the concrete Citizenship of the 14th Amendment.
And, God is the Absolute Right in the Voting Rights Act.
So because of the sowing of our ancestors,
we now reap the harvest of righteousness.
It's Libation Time.
When we trumpet the harmonic praises of our ancestors, we
are composing a symphony of praise for Jehovah.
When we celebrate the surviving rivers of our ancestors,
we are celebrating the ocean of Jehovah's power.

Griot Space

Black rainbows don't fade
but continuously grow
into God's sunshine.

A Poem for Lorenzo Thomas' Post-Modern Concerns

Where is the arbitrary line of sanity
that borders the temple of my familiar,
which is etched forever into political sand dunes
that converge endlessly on themselves,
creating a fleeting mirage of gated communities
saved by vouchers and remote controls
so that [i] may safely enjoy *The Price Is Right*
packaged neatly around "The Return of Jesus, Part XVI,"
as a pale, visually challenged messiah goes down
like Joan of Arc living in a low rent high rise,
while my critical memory faintly echoes something about
Philadelphia's Tiananmen Square Massacre,
further eroding and moving my line of sanity,
annexing more mulattos for the Nielsen Ratings?

A Texan without boots is a trope
for world cable culturalization.

Lorenzo picks up Baldwin's
dented, dusted, cobweb covered camcorder
and pushes the red button.

For whom will you witness?

Don't Call Me Angry

Don't call me angry just 'cause
[i] ain't got no mo' cheeks left to turn,
and [i] no longer want to do business
with the travel agent who sent me on that first boat ride.
Generations of generations disappeared
like soil giving way to erosion,
like a VCR in the clutches of a crack addict,
to be cashed in for a quick hit of mercantilism,
leaving our Black fields seedless and barren.
Ancient graying architects become unable to reconstruct
the umbilical bridge to manhood for fatherless boys
who feel betrayed by a ghost village unable to protect them.

Don't call me angry because [i] don't believe in Reagan's
mystical, magical market place because [i] know that
[i]'m the permanent wheel that keeps it rolling;
for [i] know that a high risk area is anywhere
Black folks live, allowing Jim Walters to charge
higher tokens based on your city code.
That's how [i] know that giving exploitation a new name
like capitalism is like putting trailer trash n a new suit;
the funk of injustice will seep through the garments.
So [i]'ve decided to get off the boxcar of integration
and ride the airliner of Afro-nationalism.

Don't call me angry when
[i] cheer for the touchdown scored by O.J. just after some
cowardly cop told me, "Move yo' ass nigger," even though
my feet were firmly planted on the soil of my porch.
But he, [i], and my grandmamma know that all the drug
boys hang out at the Dairy Bar where snow white delicacies
at the bar ain't been dairy since Domino's stop delivering
due to domestic trafficking that give a new meaning to junk
food, and its business is flowing like freeway traffic
while pliantly blind pigs and un-statesmen like councilmen
are masturbating over their petty power
to properly place stop signs in carefully chosen areas

but can't place policies to stop
the dissolution of Black people.

Don't call me angry 'cause
[i] don't care about the Baby JonBenet
when you don't care about Black Baby X.
Hell, at least Baby Benet got a name.
Or, when [i] blow off fat ass angry white militia males
who complain about niggers taking over the world
from their super-sized suburban homes with
their shotguns laying beside their big screens and their
hound dogs that walk their children to private school,
or when [i]'m called a murderer, or a rapist, or an animal
even though colonization isn't the fruit of my tree.

No acres, no mule, no workman's comp, no trademark, no
copyright, no nothing but weary over worked bodies
and under paid lint lined pockets,
and [i] can't get a heart transplant,
even though [i] invented the process.
Now who's heart-less?

For Maryemma G.

You be eating greens with yo' fingers and
making men from mules with yo' mind.
Instead of staying in the stoic, steel stiletto heels of
Eurodemia, you be grading papers in flip-flops
'cause Raven grandmas got an antiquity too.
Your sensuously swaying swagger is full with Hurston's
grapefruit; the hips on which you hang your theory are
temples—testaments to the religion of Janieism.
[i] long to consummate with your conjecture.
May [i] be baptized in the watery depths of your cerebral
and cleansed by the flowing juices of your intellect.
A cup full of your prowess be flowing
over the sides of my small calabash.
[i] sub-divide your soul like suras,
bookmarking you for my moments of need.
[i] turn the pages of you,
my mind caressing each of your tropes.
Salvation is found in Nature's bound leaves that bear
the holy fruit of your plump fancy and inspiration.
Yet, your deliverance of me
is the doorway of redemption for you.
May [i] be Tea Cake for you?; or, on the wrong day
[i] will be Wright, and we can make daemonic discourse
that will deliver Dionysus to the dreams of profane divinity,
like ebony versification raising the bowels
of white supremacy to aesthetic heights.
You be the dichotomy standing on the yin and yang
of saber-toothed womanism, or is Walker just a purple
succubus—a "Darling Nikki" in disguise?
Still, my nature demands that [i] sign the dotted line
and be rescued from my myopic phallicism.
Truth is...
[i] be a papa chicken looking to be canonized by you.
We all got a little Randall Ware that needs to be Vyricized,
making us the new Adams and the new Eves.

Blue Colored Glasses (for Pecola)

[i] am an ostrich, burying my head,
hoping that my narcotic religion will save me.
Jesus was a blonde-headed nigger
who sells me faith in a Revlon can.
Yet, even he was sold out by Uncle Tom leaders
for being too Black for men with pockets lined with silver.
Still, [i] can marry myself white or at least other;
that's what the demography form tells me.
[i] believe in American realism and *Different Strokes*.
A bundle of hair will save my soul,
as [i] trade in my scriptures for a straighten comb
and put on a pair of blue colored glasses.

[i] Can't Dance
(The Middle-Class African American Blues Song)

[i] have drained my well-rounded West Continent
bellowing laugh of its tropical ripeness.
The wet juicy fruit of my unencumbered joy
as been traded in for a well-calculated chuckle,
dropped on cue because dollars are more valuable
than yesterday's religion.
My colorless Country Club membership
will save my Black soul.
Instead of shouting to the heavens,
[i] praise God under my mumbled breath.
My flowing river of natural rhythm
has been replaced with a warehouse gray time clock
ticking to beats of Bing and Bob.
HBCUs are forgone memories of wishing [i] could
eat at the table instead of in the kitchen.
Now [i] can eat at the table just as long as the Knights
of the White Table remember to fund
an endowed Chair for me.
[i] don't need a plate.
[i]'ll eat off one of the others' after they have finished.
And to show that [i]'m really grateful and plan not to be a
burden, [i] don't even wash my dish fo' [i] use it.
That way, the State can save money on the water bill
so as [i] can have some side-dishes with my major.
[i] have a poster of MLK before he went to Memphis
and a poster of Malcolm after he went to Mecca.
[i] ain't said "What's up?" since '75,
but [i] do drop a "Dyn-o-mite" every once and a while.
[i] don't break white verbs
although [i] do burn Black bridges.
The only African [i] know is the proverb
pick-pocketed by Hillary Clinton.
[i]'m against affirmative action 'cause
[i] like being a special Negro.
[i]'ve seen things that most Blacks haven't,
like the inside of a white politicians' hip pocket.

[i]'m a proud lay-a-way Negro, laying away
until [i]'m needed for November's second Tuesday.
[i] always run the light when the man in the bow tie
tries to sell me a paper.
My family is something 'cause white folks come to our
funerals and invite us to their children's weddings.
My favorite phrase for Black folks is "you people."
[i] only went to the community Kwanza celebration 'cause
my boss sent me as a representative of the firm.
[i] gave a late speech and an early exit.
The Jesus on my wall looks like De Vinci's lover.
The Jesus in my heart looks like Charlton Heston.
And the Satan of my mind looks like Louis Farrakhan.
[i] don't dance.
Not 'cause [i] ain't got no rhythm,
but 'cause my dancing might get my jungle blood boiling
and remind me that there's life under this plastic skin,
and that won't do 'cause massa
will make me ghetto property again.

Poetry Is...

And God spoke, hurling life like a boulder
through his voice box,
"Let there be..."

Poetry is the physical mosaic
of God's portrait painted with words,
to create like a carpenter,
order like a judge,
maintain like a janitor,
and give meaning like a philosopher
to our living room.

We're all tropes or
metaphors in action.

Appreciation of You (in three Parts)

Exposition

There are no phonemes and morphemes in any vault of
words which articulate what it is that [i] feel for you.
Man has not postulated or formulated the concepts
which effectively paint how [i] am for you.
Yet my soul demands to scream silent whispers
of its gratitude for you,
so [i]'ll allow my bubbling brain to babble
like a newborn expressing its love for a mother.

I

You are my compass leading me to Psychedelica.
You are my holy script evolving me to perfection.
You are Neruda's Word that carries the DNA of life.
You are Paz's Bodies writing meaning on an empty sky.
You are Mistral's Nature making me forget
          it is difficult to die.
You are Johnson's Voice that [i] lift and sing.
You are Hughes' Ancient River that baptizes me.
You are Hurston's Pear Tree that nurtures me.
You are strawberry agape poured into human form,
          blazing into the fire of revolution,
You are
          the strength of an ox,
          the diamond of hope,
          the wisdom of Mother-Time, and
          the infinite space of Love.

II

To be without you
is to be night with no day
is to be hydrogen with no oxide
is to be Willie Tyler with no Lester
is to be Black Colleges with no serene scars of struggle

is to be human with no humanity
is to be sin with no redemption
is to be sun with no moon
is to be Earth with no water
is to even be life with no death
is to be a James Brown song with no bridge
is to be incomplete.

III

Like G.E., you bring me to life.
Like BASF, you didn't make me,
you jus' make me better.
My one single act of greatness
was being smart enough to allow you to love me.
For you make Love breathe like the air in my lungs.
The caress of your consoling cotton hands
across my tightened torso after a days work
is like erupting 1,000 times.
Upon your rock [i] build my church
as a testament to God's perfection.
[i]'m remembering the way you told that cop
that [i] wasn't afraid of him.
Your steel-steady, unwavering voice
reached deep into the depths of my viscera
pricking a fire that began to smolder in my soul
making me know that even though
[i] was about to take an ass whipping,
like Jesus on the cross
the restoration and preservation of your honor is worth
more
than all of the ass whippings that one man can endure
for my life has value
because you are the minerals that
fertilize my African soil.

The Sweetness of Life (for Walter Payton)

Walter be movin' and jukin';
he be James Brownin' on da good foot
with his brand new bag because
papa never did take no mess,
gettin' up on the down stroke
stiff-arming the Sovereignty Commission.
Walter be movin' and jukin'
like a trailblazer on the underground railroad.
He followed the freedom path from Jackson to Chi-town,
connectin' chocolate cities on that SWAC *Soul Train*
runnin' from poverty right into the Hall of Fame.
He now stands as the statuesque standard for manhood.
Like Charlie "Bird" Parker be movin' and jukin'
up and down the scales of highs and lows.
Sweetness feet be musical compositions
be-bopping Bird's notes into shotgun slugs
breakin' the cotton confines of Columbus chains.
Sweetness be the jazzy versification in a Langston poem
and the downright fluidity of Dunbar's dialect.
As Bird shape-shifted "Funny Valentine"
Sweetness re-styled Lombardi's sweep,
takin' a flat note and bendin' it
until it was acuminated into altitudinal art.
Sweetness turned running lanes into beautiful possibilities
like the kinetic colors in a Romare Bearden collage.
Sweetness feet, like Sammy's feet,
be tap dancin' in rhythmic chaos—
poundin' out beats that burst the
stoic, slow fallacy of what the body can do.
That's the unteachable technique
that time travels back to Timbuktu
like the muddy Mississippi flows back to the Congo,
swingin' and swayin' like Sweetness
survivin' Sunday morning warfare.
Like Robert Smalls navigatin' on the high seas,
Walter was dodgin' patter-rollin' linebackers
and defensive ends determined to end him;

thus, we cheered from couches to crowded stadiums,
knowing that every yard was another
small step for man, a major mark for mankind,
and a heavenly, hellacious move for the highlight reel.
With his smooth, sultry shake and swerve, Sweetness
broke mo' ankles than the mob and mo' hearts than Denzel.
Walter be movin' and jukin' like we be breakin' verbs
'cause verb breakin' represents the power of a people
whose vernacular was sacked in the end zone
from the blind side, but still gave birth to the tongue
which became America's soul-language
'cause the dialect is in ya' like culture be in yams.
With every juicy bite you can taste
the funkdafied aesthetic of bluespeople.
With every move you could feel
the vibration of his ebony antiquity.
That be Sweetness;
his body language had mo' words than *Webster*
and mo' clarity than *Hooked on Phonics*.
He was an athletic ambassador for humanity,
high-stepping and hurdling the walls of injustice
with every yard, tramplin' out the sour muscadine
grapes of Jim Crow with every first down, crushin'
under his 4.4 yard per carry feet the pale media's
malicious white lies about Black academies.
He be strivin' like Civil Rights Marchers
on their way to Washington:
one mo' yard, one mo' yard, one mo' yard,
like we be strivin' one mo' day, one mo' day, one mo' day
to pay our bills that keep blitzing us like those '85 Bears.
Yet, Walter became the bronze skinned, woolly haired
baby, who willingly scarified his gridiron life
so that he could bestow proprietorship to the people
only to be double-crossed by the
double tongue of ivory capitalism.
He be, they say, too small 'cause his school too small,
still he be the glorious second coming
of all that has come before him—
badder than Superman, he be HBCUman:

with the power of Jim Brown,
the speed of Gayle Sayers,
more elusive than O.J.,
and the highflying Houdini of Barry Sanders.
Walter be just another John the Baptist makin' the way
for HBCU homeboys to become household names.
When the dust had cleared this small man from a
small school stood 16,726 yards taller than any titan
from Mt. Div. I, proving that
the SWAC is the MAC of the NFL.
Yet Sweetness, like yams, belongs to everybody.
His hip hips made us believe in the democracy of sport.
With his "blue bengal" heart and "windy city" courage,
he made warriors of us all.
He was the rainbow of rhythm
that caused our humanity to rise like the Nile,
making fertile the hearts of man to love past their fear.
His Sunday sermons were like revivals to our souls,
for in him beat the spirit of a man possessed
with the syncopated cadence of life.
He be Sweetness, makin' our lives a bit more savory.
Even in his vivid vulnerability he managed
to be more mountain of a man than most.
Still teachin' lessons in his last days that
his true sweetness was his golden love for family
and his honeyed zest for man-kind-ness.
This be Sweetness, an exhibition of altruism in cleats.
And with those cleats,
he plotted a perfectly painted path for us
to become champions of our own destiny.

Bob Moses: Gardener of Minds

Your overalls fit you like a well woven truth,
as you have tilled the fields of our resources,
moving us from sharecroppers to social mathematicians.
You are a gardener, finding the rich minerals of the Earth
in soil left for waste by years of white erosion.
You put your hands deep into the soil of our brains
and cultivated capacious crops of communities.
You have shown us that the equation for liberation
is love + work = freedom.
You taught us that votes count if we count our votes,
that numbers are our shield and sword
in the battle for equality,
and that all voices matter if we matter to till and raise them.
With your edifying tools, you plowed our minds
and dropped seeds of the movement that swelled
in the bellies of our soul and produced fruit for the ages.
Your Algebra project projects primary numbers
to answer the call for new wheat to harvest
the next yield of mass movement.

News Anchor: "Today, a small boat with a father and his daughter overturned. During their struggle to survive, the father removed the lifejacket from the child, saving himself while allowing his daughter to plunge to her death. We will have video of this horrific scene when we return."

Me—after months of fighting with White Mississippians over Senate Bill 2236 (School Safety Act) and the HBCU Ayers Case: "Please, Gawd, don't let him be Black!"

What You Can Say in a Poem...?
(A poem for a seven year old white girl that demands to be written, even if she is white, because all the time poems are metaphors of our tropish lives)

Experience has given me more programs than [i] have channels, and my brain's network president is too busy reading polls than crafting art because [i]'ve been made a poetic paraplegic—stuck between the iron-clad definition of the thing and the liquid purpose of the thing.
The cluttered closet of my mouth needs to be cleaned, but the guerrilla army in my heart outnumbers the scientists in my mind, and the thick and crunchy theories in my mind are too dense for my teeth to dissect or my mouth to swallow.
Or, shall [i] say that the pop-culture poet in my heart dances too swiftly for the scientific scales
plotted by the part-time philosopher in my mind.
"Reality really does defy that scientific approach to life strategy," said the tragic clown as he jigged a two-step to the malfunctioning music of mass mindlessness.
[i]'m trying to get the ten pound ham
into the eight pound tray.
But if [i] cut off two pounds, [i] won't be able to feed the family—like hating you is killing me.
[i]'m like a lion that's gotten hold of a buffalo.
[i] know it's the right thing to do, but...this buffalo

30

is a bit bigger in my hands than it was in my mind.
[i] mean...which card can [i] turn, the race of spades or the
diamonds of humanity?—which is a tricky hand to be dealt
when we are being mammals who paint everything with the
dye of race as the cheap colors
bleed on and damage the fabric of our humanity.

How can crops of slaves be painted with a more baneful
hue than the crops of slave owners
who reap the emerald benefits of crimson labor?
Still, white is the billboard of honor because all is fair
in lust, capitalism, and lions dinning on antelopes; so we
chronicle magnolias crimes as random and raven crimes as
allegorical.
[i] guess it's about who owns the brush
and colonizes the colors.
But wait...isn't this about the cherub child?
Seven year old hands, trembling like puppies
abandoned along the roadside in the frozen pits of winter.
How does a child take her last breath, knowing
that daddy cared more about life's broken pieces of silver
than her tiny soul of gold?
The Renaissance really worked its three-card monte
when it painted over God with colorful capital and
sucked the marrow of ritual from the bones of art,
making way for *The Jerry Springer Show* to fill the
hollow chambers of empty wagons with no GPS.
Still, how can [i] call a man a coward
when [i]'ve never had to swim his oceans?
(This buffalo is getting away from me.)
So like our sable juggler of balls weighted with heavy
words, [i] aim to be Baldwin-like rather than a better-
Baldwin and realize that writing is merely our road map to
the truth, and that life, humanity, and civility are houses
whose fates are based on the density of the concrete
we pour.
If our foundation of truth is fractured
then the house of humanity will crumble.
So, with my razor words [i] must sink my

lion's fangs into the heart of the matter,
deep into the windpipe of this buffalo.
If we do not love our children more than life,
then life becomes a bald-faced lie told by a buffoon.
Our eyes are blinded by the plastic shine of living
as we are, like whores, sucking on the phallus of
physicality, retarding the germination of our souls'
fragile flowers.
So, let's taste the tart truth.

Some people, like a daddy who watches his child drown
in the waters of the Mississippi or in the quicksand of
poorly planned public education, do not need to be
parents—like some brothers just don't have enough game
for the big leagues or like Nixon didn't have enough juju
to administer America's affirmative action.
Maybe my optimistic soul is too far buried in the callous
core of my frozen flesh of pessimism, which needs to be
this way to withstand the wicked winds of rotten reality.
The overly brightened sun of history forces me to
cover my infantile eyes with apathetic sunglasses
and see only the gray shadows of life.

Now tell me, was her death more Juliet or Jack the Ripper
when placed on a pallet next to abortion or slavery?
Where will it be catalogued in the antiquity of evil?
Who will use it as a trope for their cause,
and will their ashy agendas be washed any cleaner?
How many rivers of subjective reality do we need to sail
'til we dock our boat at the bank which affirms that
the color of truth is...truth?

Movements in Blackness: Shades of Ideology

An African owns his own company.
A Negro works for somebody else's company.
And a nigga will steal from both.
An African magnifies history.
A Negro justifies history.
And a Nigga uses history books to
balance his coffee table and prop open a broken window.
An African writes for Nationalism.
A Negro writes for assimilation.
And a Nigga writes bad checks.
An African remakes the world.
A Negro integrates into the world.
And a Nigga survives the world like
roaches during a nuclear meltdown.
An African tries to become God.
A Negro tries to get next to God.
A Nigga tries to get next to God's collection plate.

But when Niggas do write, they tend to become Africans

An African writes for clarity and truth.
A Negro writes for aesthetics and Caucasian canonization.
A Nigga writes for rent and something to eat.

Niggas don't write on paper, they write on life,
makin' reality mo' realer,
like makin' cocaine become crack to get you mo' higher,
or makin' blue become rage,
or turning swine into a delicacy,
or turning thunderbird into a dinner wine.
Africans are griots who must scribe
the Nigga's ugly reality into a beautiful strange.
Negroes just wanna read Shakespeare,
and Niggas are just trying not to go out like McBeth.

An African is about legacy.
A Negro is about tradition.

And a Nigga is about today,
making tomorrow merely a
footnote afterthought to daily survival.

An African has vision.
A Negro has sight.
And a Nigga sees only what needs to be seen.

An African is God made.
A Negro is man made.
And a Nigga jus' wanna know what time it is.
An African embraces Blackness and rejects Whiteness.
A Negro embraces Whiteness and rejects Blackness.
And a Nigga accepts Greenness and rejects Brokenness.
An African is a humanist.
A Negro is a capitalist.
And a Nigga is an opportunist.
An African embraces the yam.
A Negro rejects the yam.
And a Nigga embraces the yam with a side of chitterlings.

An African makes love to the universe.
A Negro procreates with another being.
A Nigga fucks to make it through the night.

Index/Glossary

African: a freely flowing Pre-Colonial river
Negro: a river dammed by the bricks of Colonialism
Nigga: what floats in Colonialism's sewage system

Impotence

Fragments of flamed thought
wildly flicker in my mind.
My pen cannot come.

Equal Tears

The reservoir of my eyes flows like
the sand dunes of white knights in blue suits
after a nine millimeter lynching of an African flower.
[i] have as much sympathy for a chalky child
being dragged by a dark carjacker
as those pale boys in cobalt have for Diallo.
Sable children are dragged and lynched on a daily basis
by the Department of Education
and hunted like game by the Department of Corrections.
We need to trade our tears for bullets
and cry Black rain all over
the United Plantations of Ameriklan.

[i] Know It Was the Blood

[i] know it was the blood, raining down from the cross
covering me with red revelation, causing a fiery revolution
which led to sprouting spring of evolution,
a sweet symphony of spiritual ecstasy. Was blind but now
can see the transparent Truth even when hidden in lead lies.
Was deaf but can now hear Truth even in a gnat's wing.
Now have a river of courage
where there was once a cesspool of fear.
And with the clean ears of my soul
[i] can now hear the voice of God.
Sometimes it's a golden trumpet, blasting healing notes
from the heavens, moving majestic mountains to
the funk jam of ruby reconciliation.
Sometimes it's a lone guitar chord, stretched and bent like a
scream in the night, sounding like Hendrix on the other side
of life as free and high as he wants to be.
See, ain't nothing like being high on God,
and [i] ain't got to sell my tv to get it.
'Cause it's the mystical, melodious music of the Angles
removing the pulp of the physical from my eyes and ears.
[i] am no longer afraid to display my crimson membership
card 'cause [i] know that all that [i] am
didn't come from a creation but from the Creator.
And neither your weak weathered words nor your mosquito
light actions can keep God's message from getting through
that faith without action ain't nothing but a corpse. So, you
can pray until your knees have calluses, but if you ain't got
the courage to carry David's catapulting slingshot like a
man, ain't nothing in your pitiful, pathetic life gone change.
For faith flowers from the watering words of the *Book*.
So for the Truth you don't know where to look,
'cause you're using someone else's eyes to follow the map,
quoting scriptures you ain't never read
and wondering why your faith is so decayed and dead.
How you gon' be a Christian talking 'bout you scared:
scared to lose yo' job, scared to lose yo' friends,
scared of what yo' family gon' say.

You need to be scared of that hot river
that's gon' boil you into a sinner's soup.
[i] know that [i]'ll be the only defendant standing
before the Supreme Court on Judgment day,
and Christ is the only lawyer who can file my appeal.
For Christian means Christ-in or Christ in you.
And as long as you got fear ain't gon' ever be no Christ in
you 'cause Christ was a political prisoner
one of the earliest revolutionaries who, like all
revolutionaries, was offered up by the Uncle Tom leaders,
weak egg-shell walking men who fear man more than God,
who would bow down to Caesar's Rebel Flag
and turn their back on the pure water of the Truth.
So go ahead and get philosophical
and act like you don't fear the rod,
but if you mess with His children
you gon' get that onion thumped by God.

See, [i] know it was the blood.
It was the blood that covered Tubman's steps
It was the blood that covered Turner's ropes.
It is the blood that flows in our fight 'til death for freedom.
If we must die, let our final swing
be a grenade for the freedom of our children.
For [i] know that the Angel of the Lord
will be bathing in a blazing bright light carrying
a sword stronger and sturdier than stainless steel
in His right hand, and in His left hand
will be the Word (the seed and fertilizer of all life)
that was the mineral of the fertile soil, that became God,
that became flesh made manifest in the garden of man.
And with this steel sword and sharp Word,
the Angel of God will be swinging mighty blows,
leading the cleansed cavalry of the Lord to victory.
And [i] am the Victor because [i] now wear a crown blood.

Tree of Life (Black Colleges Be Here)

Black colleges are the water fertilizing scorched Earth,
remaining the only well from which we can
freely drink of ourselves.
Black colleges be the consistency of summer always
following the spring, removing the frigid film of frost
from the eyes of Black babies.
Black colleges be the sunshine of summer,
producing bright roses breaking through concrete,
and golden new dawns breaking through
the tight twilight of subjugation.
No matter your dusty deeds or witchcraft words,
Black colleges be the precise clocks that never stop
through budget cuts, program cuts, people cuts,
and cuts just for the sake of cutting.
But with all the chain-saw cutting by the lumberjacks
of the legislature, our legacy remains a
mighty Magnolia Tree towering high above
the cantankerous canard about Black intellect.

They run highways through our campus
like it's grand central station.
City mayors sit blinded by the greenbacks from
white palms as our deserted decor dilapidates with
the white flight of fleeing industry.
Yet, when the heavily armed State of Mississippi marched
in a merciless May on the Future of Black seeds like
misguided pesticides desperately trying to trample the
flowers of Black hope with a thunderstorm of steel rain that
poured from the funnel cloud of Governor Paul B.
Johnson's pale heart and through the lightning rods of State
issued machine guns and redneck rifles.
Seven hundred rounds were fired into the soul
of the Urban Think Tank of Mississippi.
Seven hundred steel arrows pelted screaming babies,
hanging like rag dolls from broken windows,
leaving blood saturating the campus grounds
like the sea floors of the middle passage.

And when the raging storm was finished,
leaving brick buildings shredded like Swiss cheese
and the blood of death was cleaned with the mosaic spirits
of life, and the tears were dried by the renaissance of
Southern Soul Babies, we stood on the steps of Lynch
Street and proclaimed "You missed, mutha-governor; you
missed" 'cause we be still here, here we be steel.

So vomit any venom you will; we'll still be planted here,
in this place, in this moment of time becoming the rock
upon which we built the basilica of Black intellect
steadier than half-assed affirmative action plans at
Antebellum schools that ain't never been affirmed
by Colonel Reb or Major Millsaps.
We still be the birds and bees impregnating
ebony minds with Red, Black, and Green knowledge.
We be the fertile soil for ghetto children
to plant their dreams of sovereignty.
We be the rain that washes away the dead soil of Jim Crow
and revitalizes the seeds of onyx autonomy.
We be the oxygen that flows through
the lungs of raven children.
We be the rod and the staff of Black Israelites
trapped in a Pharaoh's white Hell.
We be the Shepherds of the flock, leading them
to the green pastures of self-determination.

We might be limping like wounded liberation soldiers,
but our history gives us endless ammunition.
We might be misdirected pilots flying backwards,
but our compass is still facing the North Star of Freedom.
We might be a staggering punch drunk fighter,
but like Ali's apex, we shall rise in the last rounds
and strike a mighty death blow to ignorance,
thus defying the good ole boy back door settlement of
Ayers where Black representatives in white face
pretzelized themselves into compromising positions
so that Governor Muskrat can stand tall on the legacy of
Barnett's damning of funds from flowing into HBCU

rivers, attempting to keep our institutions as breeding
grounds for plantation labor.
With back and hands burning and straining from the whip
and the will of history we pull with every fiber in our weary
bodies to combine like cornbread and greens the
curriculums of Washington and Du Bois
in a way that illuminates emancipation that is not planted
in the wavering, fickle soil of white liberalism—
but planted in the Garvey rich soil of
one people, one aim, one destiny—to flower freedom.

We bestow BAs in Black survival.
We bestow MAs in self-love.
We bestow MBAs in collective work and responsibility.
We bestow PhDs in freedom and liberation.
So, even though clans of congressmen continue
to spit sour speech about the spoils of our legacy,
we will remain the underground railroad for children
desperately trying to escape the plantation of poorly
financed schools that rape their souls and lynch their minds.
We be the underground railroad for children whose minds
are made muddy clay by Caucasian curriculums.
We be the underground railroad for children
whose parents found freedom on the tracks of our train.
So, rifle what you will with your wayward words
our actions will continue to churn your spoiled milk
into fresh cream fortified with dark chocolate crystals.
Black colleges be here because Black minds need gardeners
who understand how to cultivate them toward the sun,
continuing to harvest Black crops that bear good fruit
so that our community can germinate alongside its lily
white counter-part and not be strangled by the weeds of
poor funding, not be eaten by the insects of unfair
admission standards, and not be baked under the heat of
improperly used test scores.
So, Black colleges remain as a greenhouse to Black
liberation as a Tree of Life for all Adams and Eves.
As long as Black people be in need, we remain
a fertile ground for flowers of freedom.

Oral Surgery

...because quite often
the sharp tongue is mightier
than the sword is strong...

Put the Ghosts to Rest (for Rainey Pool)

Confession might be good for the soul,
but it ain't good enough for a conviction,
particularly for a Greenville judge
adjudicating Pale justice on Black souls
that toil in a perpetuating purgatory
waiting on a Moses to set them free.
The scrupulous stench in the form of unsolved crimes
lingers like the smell of heated, rotten fish
because we'd rather wish them away
than undress and wash our nasty annals of Time.
A Greenwood newspaperman speaks of
a white defendant's right for a speedy trial
while selectively forgetting the right of reciprocity,
especially when that justice was delayed by an equity
system, which is a double tongued whore with both eyes
uncovered, choking on the cock of Caucasian control
as she gave the middle-finger treatment
to the children of Turner.

The Bleached Supremacy Delegation
zestfully funds *Bibles* and Lynch ropes with tax dollars—
a time of Christians crucifying prophets
in the name of Jesus and the Mississippi Way.
Now white businessmen worry about the dignity
of the matter as dignity becomes a synonym for
Antebellum commerce.
And Sam Bowers ranks with Hegel as a prophetic,
philosopher since we know more about Watergate
than about either of the Philadelphia cities.
We never notice that felony convictions and life sentences
have replaced lynchings and castrations.
No one notices how beat cop college kid killers
became the Chief of the Law and a Hinds County
Magistrate while Mrs. Rainey was questioned
about her decaying husband's neighbors
as Knight Riders went back to their day jobs
under the cover of sunlight for thirty sanitized years

until there is a surfacing of conscience—
or does shit eventually float to the top of the pool,
or does a silent fart eventually cause us
to question whose dirty deed is it.

It's libation time as Ghosts linger on the
back yard stoops of our distortedly decorated memories,
as crimson footsteps pave a walkway
to the front door of the Governor's mansion
while silent voices speak in the tongues
of those desperate to tell their own stories.
It's the Roll Call of the unrequited:
A Slave Preacher 12/11/1831
A Mississippi Reverend 5/7/1955
A WW2 Lieutenant 8/13/1955
A Fourteen Year Old Child 8/28/1955
A Brother 8/25/1959
A Farmer 9/25/1961
A Journalist 9/30/1962
A Secretarial Activist 6/12/1963
Four Junior Misses 9/15/1963
A Witness 1/31/1964
Two Brothers Walking Home 5/2/1964
Three Bus Riders in Philadelphia, Mississippi 6/21/1964
A Louisiana Peace Officer 6/2/1965
A Hattiesburg Grocer 1/10/1966
A Sixty-five Year Old Care Taker 6/10/1966
A Natchez Factory Worker 2/27/1967
A Man Walking across Jackson State University
        to Get His Wife a Sandwich 5/12/1967
A Georgia Preacher 4/4/1968
A Black Panther 12/4/1969
A High School and A College Student 5/14/1970
A Twentieth Century Escaped Slave 5/2/1973
A Pennsylvania Radio Journalist 12/9/1981

A Poem for Bennie, Byrd, and the Black Caucus: Throwing Votes into a Hollow Wind

The taste of betrayal lingers in my mouth
like rotten meat poisoning the pits of my throat.
The maggots of "go along to get along" slide like
slimy worms down my excoriated esophagus
into my burning belly, laying larva into my soul that eat
away at my memories of McComb and Montgomery*.
The smell of betrayal hovers around my nose
like a cloud of spoiled eggs; involuntarily [i] whiff
and the malfeasance engulfs me like a toe-jam sandwich
moistened with the liquid bowels of "sell-out" juice.
The touch of betrayal lunges itself deep into my soul's
viscera, shredding me like the Titanic giving way
to an iceberg of illicit invention.
The sight of betrayal plays in rewind like a seventies
blacxploitation flick, starring the Onyx Stooges:
the politician, the preacher, and the lawyer, all dressed up
to sit on Muskrat's knee and be patted lovingly.
Sit, Negroes, sit: good curs—now roll over.
"How much is that Negro politician in the window—
the one with the new Cadillac?"
The sound of betrayal plays in my fractured ears, like
Pat Boone's "Tutti Fruitti," snapping and cracking against
my cranium like the sound of Byrd trying to squeeze a
square chalky lie into a round hole of ebony truth.
The Black Caucus wears the scarlet letter of
Accommodation, as they eat at the Table
of Bennie's Boudoir, his soiled sheets wet
with the whitening promises of power.
One frosty vertical finger pressed tightly against
four sable horizontal lips 'cause the people don't
need to know that they are the plaintiffs.
Bennie the Bully bulldozes the passive poinsettias, while he
fertilizes them with the manure of "feel-good" rhetoric.
The colored Caucus is cemented to Jim Crow's Capitol
steps like ancient Knights, yet their armor is really
borrowed clichés of yesteryears, cracked like all of

integration's putrefied promises.
Sweetened shit may be sugary, but it's still excrement.
Twenty-six years did we labor, blind-folded by the State,
never did we know that it was our warriors
who had their hands on the light switch.
Daddy Muskrat and Patter-Roller Moore bark loudly
and the mutts roll-over for some dry bones of tv time.
Reuben, the obvious-traitor acting as arbitrator,
be doing what they ask of him,
his hands stained with thirty silver pieces
as he lynches the movement one arbitration at a time.
Ayers lies in the mud like a fallen Princess,
her children silently sucking on the seeds of stratagem,
as Byrd weighs like an Albatross
around the neck of Thurgood's legacy.
"Sing a song of Black Birds Baked in a Pie,
too many belly-full Negroes too afraid to die."
The caucus has made a carcass of Ayers, its body flapping
like a cadaver in the wind of liberal rhetoric as the vultures
will be 'round the second Tuesday to ask for
our continued hand in marriage
while they commit adultery with our slave masters.
As the conservative train of rollbacks keeps on a-moving,
the conductor is from Bolton—
serving up another fish fry instead of freedom.
The winds of change knock heavily on the fragile doors of
HBCUs, opening themselves to midnight Trojan Horses:
"Beware of Negro Politicians bearing gifts."
Jake Ayers rolls over like a betrayed solider;
we spit on his name, washing our hands
in the bloody waters of JSC 1970—
but the niggers didn't die 'til they believed in
Bennie(dick-us) Arnold.

*Montgomery County Mississippi

Chivalry, Sexism, or Revolution?

Is it wrong to say
that Black women want to be
rescued by Black Knights?

Music Is

Music is the palpitating, pulsating
personification of God's voice.
It is the middle C of the universe.
It is the baritone beating of humanity's red organ, marking
time through the revolving door intervals of life and death.
That last beat skyrocketing you into
the holiest heights of the great beyond.
It is the falsetto of melodic mocking birds, boozing blue
jays, and rocking robins swaying the branches
of life's tree ciphering their muse of improvisation
from loaded blueberries.
It is the alto of winds rustling wildly
through magnolias or waves smacking
beach backsides during seaside salvation.
It is the thunderous bass of lighting, snapping and crackling
like new songs in the ears of old listeners.
It is the Theloniously silent space played at intervals,
between the upbeat of what we think and
the downbeat of what we do.
It is the well-regulated four bar blues of
four seasons marking the time of man.
It is the never-ending, circular seven day scale,
which keeps flowers growing despite the tragic opera of
street sweepers, freebasers, and hungry bleeding bellies.
It is involuntary tears raging and rolling
like damned up rivers unable to be damned up any longer.
It is the sacred and the profane fornicating and
consummating at the same time, in the same time,
and on the same beat.
It is the tense but fluid dichotomy of being X and Y.
It is the fire that fuels the constant flaming question
of why we are here, and did we come to get down.
It is the voice of heaven shinning a light in the cave of hell.
It is God providing the talent,
and turmoil providing the opportunity to be great,
where sexual healing cures spiritual afflictions
and public enemies sample purple passions

because we're all entrapped in the body politic.
It is the collective call of the ancestors
and the novel response of the individual.
It is the civil war between form and soul
where a regulated, mathematical left hand fights a
rhythmic war with an emotionally liberated right hand.

Music is the keeper and conductor of our tears,
organizing our blues and jubilees for a cathartic
waterfall over the resistant bedrock of stoicism.
It is the sperm on the eggs of our lives.
It is the dance of departing as we are arriving
and the symphonic jazzification of a rocking life.
It is African phonemes housed in European syntax
creating colorful semantics with a rainbow language.
Music is the secret vernacular of an old woman
with crusty knees and sandpaper hands
whispering volcanically to a God who rests
 in the pit of her heart and sings her a lullaby
of earthly peace and a heavenly mansion.

Music is life's lifeline back to itself,
where a Wonder named Stevie can make popular
the beat of Sable arts by staying focused on the *key of life*,
while a scraggly voiced rolling stone from Minneapolis
can proclaim a wavy haired brown-eyed boy from Detroit
as America's greatest bard.
Where an androgynous King Richard of Macon
can give birth to two sons:
the hardest working Soul Brother on the planet
and a Voodoo Chile in an acid red house.
It is where muddy waters can give birth to rolling stones.
Where an inspirational, instrumental love supreme
can give birth to a verbal movement of Ebony arts.
Where the Nutbush Tennessee Queen of Rock
can shine a light for Detroit's Queen of Soul.
Where "baby, baby" can be
as spiritually profound as "lawd, lawd."
Where Solomon's Son can anthologize

a book of singing shepherd's blues.
Where Highway 61 and Highway 49 became the womb,
so a whole nation of Reconstruction's illegitimate children
can purge their souls of spoiled promises.
Where royalty rises regally from the bowels
of serfs and slaves, welding work songs into
spirituals and weaving blues into gospels.
As N'awlins began to swing,
Harlem's New Negro began to bop.
Then a white boy with a funny name was
anointed with the blood of backwoods gospels,
shook his pale ass on two-tone television,
to free every Confederate in the world from the
crippling cancer of their xenophobic lullabies
only to be sacrificed at their altar of fear and greed.
Where Motown ambassadors
were the first freedom riders.
Where otherness is the mainstream.
Where Delta pains can create English Beat-tales.
Only with music can you be
Black on the radio and white on the video,
and a PWT can gain a voice through ghetto versification.
For music can take our well-defined Blacks and whites
and create a kaleidoscope of beautifully blended grays
that give life to Roy G. Biv and his endless possibilities
despite our fears that make us unnaturally monochromatic.

If pale peacock is an oxymoron, then music lets us know
that racism is as unnatural as a tiger hating its stripes
or a leopard bleaching its spots to hang with the lions.

What is music?
It is when poisoned integration produces hip-hopping
revolutionaries pissed off about being lied to again,
as their stinging words are heavy with the baggage of their
parent's broken dreams, and bad checks are now sharpened
urban daggers that pierce America's gut like crushed glass
in our baby food, cutting our insides like shrapnel.
Yet, rap becomes the fertile vomit that can fertilize our

evolution if we can get past the stank bitterness of the
belly's natural regurgitation of a spoiled age.
What is music? It is the Truth that hides inside our lies—
our Freudian slips that slide down our hierarchy of needs.
It is our melodic memories of yesterday jams
and our syncopated hope of future grooves
bridged by our reverberating riffs of surviving today.
It is the light of our day and the Black of our night.
It is the if in L.I.F.E. that fertilizes reality into
an endless butterfly effect so that we may briefly
commune with our utopian selves and sleep better
while passing through this physical perdition.

Census Blues

They are counting us
to figure how many mo'
jails they need to build.

Revelations of a Bastard Child

Who's the mother fornicator?
Make my reservation for the State Hospital;
white knowledge jackhammered into a Black brain
will make anybody mental.
[i] like to learn but not about me, you can't get
waste from white, but we all come from Greece?
Double Consciousness is a jack-in-the box
euphemism for Schizophrenia;
See, [i]'ll be Black long as [i] ain't from Africa.
'Cause the games we play are built on a sliding scale,
wanted to flip flop the rules the first time
O. J. didn't go to jail.
You fight to keep a li'l white kid with a knife
from being sent home
but quick to wave the white flag of federal charges against
Black students for throwing popcorn?
As people on cocaine continue to get more slack,
though cocaine is the testicle that ejaculates crack.
Police officers kill college kids and are patriotically
painted into the purified robes of judges
as proper procedure is a sweet seductive synonym for
unloading your weapon on an unarmed man.
[i] wonder what Black people gon' do
when the Constitution finally hits the fan.
You slyly speak out for Satan's State's rights
'cause you remember that the Klan crept in like locus
as Federal Troops rolled out under the cover of the night.
The Hayes-Tilden Compromise smells of the same funk
as the Berlin Conference Proclamation.
When Black folks gon' get to provide some colors
in the family portrait of our emancipation?
Better yet, let me and my partners walk into Rome
and start dividing up yo' crib like it's our home.
Dollars for hard times is called welfare for the wretched
rags when it's given to brothas and sistas
but it's Colgate's cooperate assistance
when it's given to Chrysler,

like it's theft when a brother does it
but embezzlement when done by a sallow shyster.
Like Michael Jordan has great natural abilities,
but John Stockton is a heady player.
Like Jimi Hendrix was a drug addict,
but Elvis Presley had a sleeping disorder.
You became mediocre mid-town medical geniuses
by using Red and Black hunters and farmers as lab mice.
Your pasty technology has killed one hundred million
colorful bodies, but you can't cure the common cold?
You have gift wrapped freedom for everybody
except your slaves.
The proof of your crystal stairway to a higher civilization
is that you can cannibalize mass destruction?
How you gon' arrest me for carjacking a Cadillac
when y'all jacked a whole continent?
Black people supposed to be America's worst sin,
but [i] ain't never known a brotha
who blew up a government building.
Can't get into college 'cause [i] can't pass the ACT
'cause it's my fault ain't none of the stick-figure teachers
qualified to teach me.
My suffering is worse than a contagious leper,
[i] got a disease called taught by an uncertified teacher.
You give China and Cuba failing grades on human rights,
but your Civil Rights GPA
should have you on academic probation.
You sell weaponry to Iran and train Saddam
with taxes taken from textbook money,
then get pissed off when he sodomized you
with the nuclear rod you gave him,
especially since you were planning to rape him
like the rest of your backhouse wenches
who give you head for sugar and wheat.
If Africans are uncivilized creatures at war,
is the tribal warfare any more civilized
when it's in Kosovo?
Nat Turner fights for his liberation, and he gets hung.
White folks commit treason and get a flag and a song.

[i]'m tired of your little white lies
staining and soiling my big, Black brain.
[i] feel like putting my big Black foot
in yo' tight, white anal retentive ideology.
But [i] turn the other cheek
because of my borrowed and burned ashen theology.
Aristotle's only lie is about the color of the Egyptians
since Leonardo Da Vinci's brush can't paint bronze skin.
Red, white, and blue eyes remain dry
while Black violets wither off the vine,
yet we come in heavy blue waves out patriotic bleeding
eyes for the white magnolias at Columbine.
My education demands that [i] carry
a hammer and nails to build my own back door.
[i] ain't gon' reach the sky if my eyes are
nailed and glued to the floor.
They say its better to fly like backwards birds
and have a story to tell.
[i] say its better to go down swinging
and be resurrected from this Hell.

For Hollis and His Southern Echo...

Your life is a *Freedom Song*
played in a spiraling wind that drips along
a magnolia breeze soaked with evening storm clouds
rolling over Jim Crow levies;
"Ain't scared of nobody 'cause [i] want my freedom..."
Like the water we drink,
we live off royalties from your sweat,
and we find home by the crimson blueprint of your steps—
narrow, straight, and lonely is the way of truth-telling,
but bright is the path that you have illuminated for us.
Like a grade school teacher, you are correcting our wrongs.
With the fertilizer of history, you nurture our ebony seeds.
Your legacy is a resounding Southern Echo that
reverberates through the heart of Dixie like a steel dagger.
Like Maytag and Whirlpool, you are an agitator for justice,
washing the dirt of domination and control
from the dingy ideology of America.
"[i]'ll organize 'cause [i] want my freedom..."
You helped to make crooked lines straight by lending your
voice to the re-drawing of geographic power pictures.
Like a bloody lamb, you bore the cross of incarceration so
that we may drink from the cup of liberty more abundantly.
The twelfth disciple of a McComb messiah,
you helped turn non-violence into a mighty weapon
to slay the Dragons of Dixie.
You were there at the première
of Woolworth's Opening Act.
Inside, your thoughts and emotions were wrestling
like two weather fronts, knowing you had to act illegally
to get some justice, as the weight of Ma and Pa
stood steadily on your shoulders
like shadows of history creeping into a new Dawn.
You waited for breakfast,
knowing your meal would be a penitentiary omelet.
But you ate your fill so that we
may eat from the pie of freedom.
"[i]'ll tell the truth 'cause [i] want my freedom..."

A tongue like a switch blade and a mind like bullwhip,
you've shredded more white lies
than a tobacco company executive.
Your feet have walked up the backside of colonization.
Your eyes have seen through
the malaised mirrors of conservatism.
Your hands have coddled babies from
the smoking fire of Johnny Reb.
Your smile has beamed a baptizing glow of affirmation
that all is well when we walk like Job,
wrapped with the garment of Truth.
Tomorrow's flowers will grow tall
as they take communion from the roots of your tree,
and are saturated with your nectar,
so they can continue to pollinate the movement.

Religion Haiku

Religion is a
blanket that covers the truth
that man abhors God.

The Preamble to the Homeless Constitution
(Delivered just Days before the Homeless Uprising
which became the Homeless Revolution)

We, the homeless, promise
to seek out a Sears or J. C. Penny every night,
bust all the windows, and wait for the police
to take us to jail, for we refuse to sleep outside
the air-conditioned dream again.
We also promise to do this around four p.m.,
since, in jail, they stop serving dinner at five p.m.
And finally, we promise to live by the words
of some of our greatest homeless leaders.

Kwame Stokely Homeless:
we must unite and organize under homeless power.
Homeless Karenga:
A homeless crisis is a culture crisis.
Homeless McKay:
If we must be homeless,
let us defiantly burn the homes
of those who dragged us away from ours.
Brother Minister Louis Homeless:
Look the blue-eyed homewrecka in his optic receiver
and say,
"[i] know you stole my mortgage when [i] wasn't looking."
Jesse Homeless:
There can be no reconciliation without co-habitation;
we can no longer suffer this humiliation
of homeless degradation.
Homeless Garvey:
Just like Africa for the African,
we need homes for the homeless.
Homeless X:
And we, the homeless people of the world,
plan to gain some domicile by any means necessary.
Martin Luther Homeless:
[i] have a dream that one day
homeless boys and homeless girls

will have green grass and sufficient funds...
And [i] want you to know that [i]'ve seen HUD,
and though [i] may not get there with you,
we, as a people, will get some homes of our own.
Then we will sing in that great Negro spiritual,
"[i]'m an occupant at last; [i]'m an occupant at last.
Thank God a'mighty, [i]'m an occupant at last."

How Do [i] Describe?

My mind is bankrupt of words to describe what it is [i] feel
when [i] watch a Black woman waltz like rocking waves
away. Or, what words can [i] shape to paint
the feeling of coming home after work to a house
smelling like Sunday dinner on a Wednesday evening.
Or, what phrase can [i] turn to photograph the feeling of
your genial hand gently stroking my neck and spine
in the deep sanctity of the night.
To watch you walk up a flight of stairs
is to feel myself ascending into heaven.
How do [i] characterize the intoxication of smelling you—
not your perfume, but your natural pheromone
dripping like strawberry flavored rain baptizing me
in the aroma of you, washing away my sins of humanity.
[i] inhale your essence in the mist of you.
Wine is too weak to describe your smell and your power.
You are more like E&J and Everclear—
mixed, heated, and poured slowly over chocolate.
[i] don't know whether to drink you or eat you.
What are you to me? How do [i] illustrate,
not the erection, but the moment just before the erection.
What is that space of swirling creativity?
How do [i] know when you walk into a room
that [i]'m about to be broke.
And every man has been broke and
happy at least once in his life.
And we don't know why. We just happy to be happy.
So, [i] apologize for being unable to give birth to the words
that sculpt the solid emotions that [i] feel
when my weary watery eyes fall upon you,
when my wide-open nose whiffs you,
when my tired, trembling hands rub against you.
What is that moment of mounting tension?
[i] don't know, but let's keep doing it
until [i] find out what it is.

Mississippi's Millennium Education
(separated and fornicated)

How did the li'l red school house
become a wait station for the penitentiary,
as the principal has metamorphosed into a warden,
while hall monitors now have
color screens and nine millimeters?
A shakedown or a strip search
replaces breakfast as the first order of the day, just before
the three R's that we never get 'round to teaching.
Social-Darwinism has planted its flag into the soil
of the sixth grade under the cover of neo-Apartheid,
enforced by Mike "Negroes can't do nothing for me but
shine my shoes, fill my jails, and vote for me" Moore,
while tobacco warfare makes him a hero
as under the table he cuts deals to give
Black children brain cancer from spoiled curriculums.
He's a true patteroller patrolling the plantations
for minds not yet poisoned by public policy.
Middle school is a AAA farm club for Parchman
'cause pale teachers still mad about Brown
feed ebony children excrement disguised as daily lesson
plans, which are used to lessen the plans of ebony children
while the Tunica County Board of Supervisors invokes
separate but equal under the guise of economic expansion,
living high off the hog of river boat gaming while the
funding for the "other" residents come up snake eyes.
Thirty million in reserve but the waters don't flow south
'cause they still damned by the Jim Crow reservoir
with a Fordice pad lock, and a Judge Biggers chain.
Gambling has come to town and the only people crapping
out are the onyx residents as overseers dressed up as
college/career counselors persuade Du Bois' Talented
Tenth that the army is for them as "public school" becomes
a synonym for T. S. Eliot's "Sewer Mecca"
'cause li'l Leroy and all his friends are suspended for
truancy (the white hot irony of it all)
while blazing Bilbo words burning with bitterness

are etched into existence one expulsion at a time.
Now the Vouchers for all new Charters read:
"Privately Segregated by Public Funds,"
which is merely a synonym for "Frosted Folks Only."

Redistricting Blues

Black main can't draw no
congressional district lines
'cause de white main say
he ain't got de right ink in his pen.

Get Yo' Child a Library Card
(Warning from a Lost Negro)

Shut up. Chain your lips closed.
My friends are like dry dust in the wind,
but [i]'ve got to water the rocks with my words
in hope that sanity can bloom anywhere.
Sometimes we have to say things, give voice to the
ideas and notions rattling around in our heads
like loose bearings in squeaky tires.
If we don't, that nagging noise will spin you drunk.
It's not pitiful that [i]'m a fake.
It's pitiful that [i] want to be baptized
in the sugar of sympathy for not being able to stand
the smell of my dried fish falseness.
[i] wanted to be a flaming star, (can u dig that?)
dressed myself up in the rented language
and second-hand clothing of a star.
Wanted to be Purple Royalty.
He was my Jesus Christ Superstar,
so [i] got a perm and some pretty shirts
and fashioned my own ghetto sanctuary,
with clothes made from off the rack fabric
that tore in two weeks. That's a star's life.
The fabric of their work can't stand the strain
of the hot lights of critique.
But couldn't sing a lick and couldn't play dead,
so [i] was stuck with some lazy lyrics and
no musical air freshener to hide the smell.
Then [i] saw a poet open for Patti LaBelle,
saw the crowd go wild and began to play the role of
an overnight, internet poet until the voices of ancient winds
brought my straw house down.
And what's left,
[i]'m a fat artist formerly known as a wanna be poet
with a bad process and clothes left over
from the decade of decadence
that burn the bright reflection of
a delusional neo-plantation Negro

who believes that individuality is a religion.
See what happens when you don't read.
Get yo' child a library card.
And if you don't have any children,
don't make any until you get a library card.
In fact, don't do no mo' horizontal humping
'til you get a library card.

Much to Do About Marginalization

"Meaning is fixed by syntax," said the New Critic
as he used the bent stolen knife of his intellect
to carve out a niche for himself in Saussure's universe,
which is devoid of Neruda's "Word"
because *Critical Theory Since Plato* is a political treaty that
affirms "critical theory" is a synonym for "cultural
warfare," and "Plato" is an all encompassing trope for
"white supremacy" like a one size fits all sweater
that's unraveling at the edges because
French suits aren't cut for African hips.
Structuralism is the science of exclusion since the sentences
of life have but one reading—all turning on the axis of pale
universality. Isn't the "play" innately communicative?
If man's joy is in seeing the recognition of himself,
have we not the right to place forced foreign morphemes
into familiar syntactical positions for our own semantics?
Yet what about satisfaction, or satisfactory articulation,
which is derived from the ejaculation of precise words—
the sex of effective articulation?
But what makes "good" sex, especially since
the womb of "good" is "useful"?
Do we then have "useful sex"?
Or, are our ears too chalky to hear
the Truth of Onyx Aesthetics?
So goes language into the white abyss of arbitrariness.
Adam has a definite he wants to share.
Does the molecular nature of meaning resolve us of our
responsibility to hit the nail on the head?—
that is, find the G spot of communication?
Is Reed's syncretic approach a bridge to meaning,
a torch for language's darkness, or a blinding light for the
academic roaches who hide under the night of universality.
Can you tell me how to get to "da stow"?
Well, no wonder we can't hear God—or His falling tree.
There is too much letter and not enough spirit.

Do We Believe in Nature?

Moments before a forlorn, restless ocean pushes itself in
huge, massive waves against the fragile brown of the
beach, does it form a committee over its action?
That is—is an orgasm an innate, involuntary, biological
action like blood coursing through veins knowing where its
going like salmons spawning?
Is the thought of arousal
a flash of lightening that becomes a poem,
or are we simply like scientists
plotting the behavior pattern of the body?
Is it natural—the manner in which the waves attempt
to get as far landward as possible
like it is for me to get as deep inward as possible?
Are we really surprised that a breeze at just the right
velocity, grazing gently on our skin causes a mountainous
rising just as buds do open to the Sun's kisses?
Are we truly astonished that a nightingale's call
resting softly atop a meandering zephyr
beckons us to remember moans whispered loudly
in vividly darkened bedrooms?
Or do we realize that it's natural for gravity
to force rain drops to the center of the Earth?
What do we truly make of the moon's affect on the tide,
or the Sun's ability to sweet talk a violet into
opening her petals.
Is this seduction or nature?
The Earth does not psycho-analyze its spring
...and neither should we.

The Poison of Integration

LBJ's concept of "integration"
is an oxymoron of sweet failure at best,
a paradox or soured strawberries in the least,
a suitcase for the Negro's mis-education,
a Trojan Horse for the Negro's self hatred.

We want the right to extort millions
and serve time at the Country Club Inn.
We want the right to buy officials
and keep them in our hip pockets.
Yet our petty change can only afford petty officials
and our pockets have holes in them.
We want the right to muddy the waters of the white race.
We want the right to fornicate over Niggas like white folks.
We want the right to stab and shoot white boys
with the consistency and regularity of Black boys
and get the same hotel-jail reservation.
We want the right to paint Black folks with Nigga colors.
We want the right to own our own Niggas under
the illusion of free enterprise in our own fascist factories.
We want the right of our deeds to smell
of the same decay as white defecation.
We want an equal opportunity to go to hell.
Searching for freedom we are now decomposing from
our soiled souls from having lain in the bed
and contracting the disease of our oppressor.
Integration was never a synonym for freedom,
and desegregation was lost like a dime store toy.

Truth Haiku

Truth is a dagger
that cuts through my facade and
leaves the lie of me

No Revolution Today

The Black Revolution is held hostage
in the dazzling white straight jacket of integration
within the asylum of assimilation.
Let's be real.
Slaves with jobs and a dental plan don't storm the capital.
We write well articulated letters to editors of white owned
newspapers carrying on our clanging chatter of
discontentment with their coverage of Negro issues.
But we'll never throw a Molotov cocktail
through the window of the *Clarion Liar.*
That's uncivilized.
Yet we never question the civility of colonization
'cause enough of us are inebriated on the stupefacient of
capitalism's tokenism, spending our time chasing that high
instead of chasing freedom.
For us don't want to be free.
Us just want to be employed.
And as long as they giving jobs to one-third of us,
and incarcerating and infecting one-third of us,
the other one-third will have to start the revolution
by killing the middle class Cornball Wardly by the gate.
But until then the invisible by-lines
of the *Washington Post* will read,
"Welfare lines packed with neo-Negroes
who have fallen off the family tree of nationalism
as onyx truancy remains at an all time high.
The Ameriklan Dream is safe.
No Revolution Again today."

2G (Another Millennium Poem)

Why we so worried 'bout 2G while we still wallowing
like swine in the excrement of 1G's history.
The color line still binds our brains
like rusty, dirt colored Antebellum chains.
Trying to get to the future before reconciling your past
is like buying a car when you can't afford the gas,
or like putting on clean draws before washing your ass.
A new coat of paint can hide old wood,
but it doesn't make it any stronger,
like age isn't the only parent to wisdom.
The mere reality of a Y2K bug is a trope
of man's innate ability to dry up a wet dream,
or the foolishness of creating an animal
to be a biodegradable garbage can,
then turning around and making a ham sandwich from it.
Trying to kiss the sky with marijuana is like
trying to call God with BellSouth,
your modem is not transcendentally compliant.
Time's only value is how you spend it,
and evolution means more than going to the moon
or the ability to terminate masses like termites.
We have grown out but not up
for we have invested in everything but our souls,
putting more into the bank of man than the bank of God.
You can take the man out of the millennium,
but can you take the millennium out of the man?
Or, will he impregnate 2G with his
still stank, spoiled, pus filled sperm?

Oh yeah, happy new year.

The Cruelest Thing (for Kysha N. Brown)

Don't swim up a sista's stream causing her to confuse
your sundry summer soak for a baptism.
Don't furnish her with flags of fellowship,
especially when you know that
this act of painting love portraits is her
last attempt at salvation.
Don't pump her full of possibilities
designed to disintegrate the safety-belt of sanity
that fastens her mind to her body
and exist, if only temporarily,
in a state of spring and ice cream bliss,
only to come down to a wet soul
and an abandoned body of condemned promises.
Don't make love to women you don't love.
For when you do, you lie.

My People

My people can't be found in paper spaces
where revolution can be pimped and pretzelized
for soda pop and clothing ads,
where soul can be sucked dry for form,
and greenbacks weigh more than Black sensibilities.
My people unload trucks and drop fries at night, so they
can pick up knowledge to load their AK-47 brains by day.
My people don't lose their common sense
when they earn uncommon degrees.
My people take turns sitting up with Ms. Rosie during
her last days then spend a lifetime keeping her alive
in the safety-deposit memories of their children.
My people are most times too busy crafting culture to stand
around soundly signifying and studying its specificity.
My people sop gravy with their fingers
after building a nation with their hands.
My people live by CP time 'cause they got jobs
that bear no fruit from a limp and impotent education.
That's why we don't care four cents or
a flying flip about you or your time clock.
We'll get there when we be there.
My people sing songs to keep from killing
and kill when they have no more songs to sing.
My people get plundered constantly by the long
hard johnson of capitalism and impregnated with
the con of colonialism, so they masturbate to
reality television to euthanize the pain.
My people rage against the machine
even when they are pistons in the engine.
My people live in the bottoms 'cause it's a muddy climb to
the top of the hill, and even when you change your clothes
the pseudo pristine people only remember your dirt.
My people know the blues is the salt in the tears of music,
and that ripe gospel is found at Greater Mount Calvary New
Hope Cove Bethel Rising Star Missionary Baptist Church.
My people know that keeping it real
is being the manure at the white man's job
so that their children can flower toward the sun.

Sex Poem

Do you really want a sex poem—
words that cause your cerebral to salivate,
slyly unlocking the door to your Freudian enclave
or poking holes in the dam of your tactfulness,
releasing the waters of your proclivity?

Do you really want a sex poem?
Do you really want me to cause your brain to erupt
and send thoughts dripping down your spine,
causing an involuntary crossing of your legs
and patting of your foot,
tapping to the drum roll of your desire?

Do you really want a sex poem,
where fantasy becomes a doorway
to dogmatism disguised as honesty,
and tongues waggle wetly as metaphors
for want we want but our lips remain glued by fear?

Do you really want a sex poem,
where [i] put my words in your ear
like my phallus in the hole of your female-hood,
giving you liquid on the brain,
intoxicating and clouding your thoughts
in a haze of mental masturbation for the sake of escapism?
Do you really, really want a sex poem?
O. k., here's your sex poem.

Black people get fucked by America on a daily basis.

[i]'m Sick of Blues Poets

[i]'m sick of blues poets who ain't never seen heat
monkeys jumping while the sun sets on the flapjack flat
Delta where the skillet causes cotton to open like popcorn.
You know blues poets who write about northern urban
decay as if this no shoe wearing, sugar cane eating country
boy gives two cotton seeds 'bout urban decay.
[i]'m sick of blues poets who think
Chicago got some claim on the blues
just 'cause white folks go to all their festivals
but can't tell you that the crossroad is really
Highway 49 making a devil's deal with Highway 61.
[i]'m sick of blues poets who think that
they are as authentic as Delta dirt,
but ain't never took the time to write their name
in the mud by the Sunflower River.
[i]'m sick of blues poets who wear their name like a credit
card and act like a Gatekeeper instead of a blues teacher,
so scared to share the two line riffs
that they stole from somebody else.
[i]'m sick of blues poets who don't understand
that you "have" the blues as in being infected
with the virus of bad times;
you don't "own" the blues as in something
you purchase from a souvenir shop.
[i]'m sick of blues poets who too educated to read in cafés
yet wanna claim they were at the Do Drop In Café in
Harlem when the water broke and gave birth
to a Moving River of Black Arts.
[i]'m sick of blues poets who claim to be funky
but ain't willing to step into any shit.

[i]'m a blues poet 'cause [i]'m so country
that [i] can look up a hen's ass
and tell you how much next season's eggs gon' cost.
[i]'m a blues poet 'cause
[i] had a three piece navy blue Easter suit with brown shoes
that we got out of lay-away two days before Easter.

[i]'m a blues poet 'cause the library in my
neighborhood had more workers than it had books.
[i]'m a blues poet 'cause
[i] know that red clay can be a delicacy.
[i]'m a blues poet 'cause
my school clothes have always been somebody else's
left over play clothes that were too tight the day [i] got 'em.
[i]'m a blues poet 'cause [i] understand that
ain't no keepers of the Gate,
only man and his muddy deeds that we wade knee deep in,
constantly trying to get to the River Jordan
while trying to keep our head just one nostril above the
stench.

All Black poets are blues poets, unless
they think the blues comes with an application process.

Ms. Betty: A Silent Warrior

You fought battles that none of us wanted to,
silencing the lies about us one room at a time.
With your dust rag, you wiped away dirty deeds done to us.
With your broom, you swept away white supremacy.
With your mop, you gave our foundation
a glow that made us glisten like diamonds.
With your polish, you gave us a shine bright enough to
blind the dingy mendacity of Hollywood.
You are a living proverb of how
we got over the Mountain of Jim Crow.
For 360 months you shined like the sun, showing that
humanity is not something worn like a name brand,
but is the gold of your soul that illuminates so brightly
that America's soiled past can't dull your value.
Trusting in the crimson covenant with every fiber of your
being, leaning only to the understanding that God will
deliver us like a Washer-woman Tubman delivering slaves
across Pharaoh's filthy Red Sea if we but acknowledge
Him as the Clorox and glass cleaner of our lives.
Like Jesus' Magdalene, you baptized our feet
so that we may stand on immaculate ground.
You are a saucy sweet psalm, singing salvation songs as
God was the 1000 watt light bulb unto your path,
the concrete of your foundation, and the steel courage
of your shining shield.
With your bent back, you stood taller than Pilate.
Never in a hurry for man's riches, you waited on the Lord,
soaking your troubles in His cleansing dishwater.
You are an affidavit that we can clean all of life's evil
grime through God's Holy Bleach.

To Charlie

[i]'ve spent my last few months
with my brain in a book—
a twelve-step writer,
fighting the addiction of spoken word.
Like any junky getting clean,
without the film of instant gratification,
[i]'m sober to how drunk with pop-adulation
[i] really was.

Chasing you is like trying to catch a sunset.

From time to time
[i] find myself falling off the wagon,
longing for an amplified iron phallus.
[i]'m looking for Medina's sponge
instead of filling my own,
trying to get a quick fix to being
intelligent.
[i]'m even tempted by the
pale yellow glow of Quick Know.

Then [i] stop and just turn the page
of the book [i]'m reading and take comfort
in knowing that
one page worth of knowledge
is better than a library of lies...

Don't Pick the Fruit too Soon
(for the Guilelessness of a Pear Tree's Puberty)

All spring time fruit is not ready
to be plucked from the vine and devoured whole.
Some fruits need additional moments
under the ripening rays of sunlight.
Very few fruits can be harvested as soon as green bananas.
Additives in our diets cause our fruit to flourish too soon.
The shell is in full bloom but the pith is still embryonic.
We've become sick with our diet
of premature fruits, slyly snatched from their safe
protective pastures, whose juices
flow scantly, leaving our fields populated
with half eating cores, lying discarded in the dirt decaying
from the enlarged insects of life clawing out
their souls in a pumping motion.

A Ghetto Sunday

Sunday mornings are like fleeting rainbows—the few
slumber-still times you can hear the birds bursting into
song over the subsided clang of ghetto harmonies
as children play fearlessly under
the fragile cover of cease fire.
If you listen closely, you can hear
the deep exhales of weary weekend warriors
who made it through another Saturday night.
In the midst of this, Monica makes yams.
Like snowballs surviving a Mississippi summer,
the aroma of sweet roses pushes through the residue
of crack pipe and gun smoke,
filling the air with the tangerine pheromone
of Nature's will to survive.

We Be Ground Gods

We be ground gods we be.
[i] came here as an Adamite
until [i] fornicated with a cherubim
in a fire-engine dress which rebirth me as Enos.
Yet Eloheem kept His eyes on me and
found favor with my third life,
shut me up in a hermitage for forty days and forty nights,
and [i] was re-baptized and restored.
We be ground gods we be

Able to do greater things than He who defeated Death.
[i] keep giving birth to myself
hoping to evolve back to my plurality.
We be ground gods we be.
If it be true that we be made in the image,
is William Tyndal or Yahweh
the potter of your clay and the author of your play?
The Swan of Stratford-upon-Avon
constructed a Globe Theatre from Hebrew scriptures
to conduct one act comedies and tragedies with no
survivors because we don't know that
we be ground gods we be.
For Satan is Prince of the air.
Do you give him feet to walk upon the Earth?
An exorcism ain't nothing but an ass whipping.
Do we need to go a couple of rounds?
We be ground gods we be,
soldiers for the second coming.
Our seed is of the seed that creates immortality,
preparing a way back to platinum perfection.
We be ground gods we be.
Believing in our mortality is our greatest sin.

Temptation in Haiku Movements

Hell is a blissed place
to dispose of a lifetime
for one flash with you.

[i] succumb to you
like the famished to spoiled food,
like Tom to white oaths.

My red organ comes
by screaming whispers of you
that fall on my soul.

You translucent lark
with a spiral crimson beak
leaving paths of gore.

You feed rapidly,
my soul gutted for diet,
left as excrement.

For Imperfect People (Joe Starks' Lament)

Falling in love is acknowledging that
we need back rubs to survive.
Marriage emerges from the ripe realization
that nobody can rub my back
the way that you can.
Forgiveness is knowing that there are no perfect hands.

Come Home

Come home to the licorice smell of rich soil
where self-determined butterflies escape
the concrete cocoons of America and
unify into the solid, onyx, marble fist of Nia.
Come home to where the sweet potato of Imani
is an aroma that seeps deep into the bowels of man
connecting him with his deeper deity.
Come home to where the interstate of Ujima
crosses the highway of Ujamma
and forms the intersection of Kujichagulia.
Let Kwanzaa baptize you like
a Mississippi Delta revival and put some juju in you.
Come home to Kwanzaa.
Come home to you.

This Is not a Protest Poem

This is not a protest poem
because [i]'ll let it be sweetened like tea to get published
because stainless steel substance is
secondary to strawberry flavored style and
scientific, surgical skill is secondary
to the dime-store magic of acceptance,
and everything is secondary to paying the rent
and living next to people who used to own you.

This is not a protest poem because
we think that God can be cashed in
on the first and the fifteenth and that
love can be put on lay-away while we be
on our knees and backs laying-away our
lives taking the iron shaft of colonialism
up our pimped-out morals as we allow ourselves
to be impregnated with self-aversion stemming from
the bright hot light of the "white normative gaze."

This is not a protest poem because organic to protest is
divorce, and [i] keep ignoring the irreconcilable differences
between me and my counterfeit country because [i] love
chicken, Cadallics, and coochie more than
the clean air of autonomy,
and [i]'ll swap my freedom for a job,
        sell my liberation for a car,
        barter and my self-determination for a 403(b) plan.

This is not a protest poem
because [i] have not sat in the sun with ebony babies
playing ABC's, 123's, and momma may [i] if u please.
And [i] have not told a Black boy that he is an apple,
and [i] have not told a Black girl that she is a flower
not with my empty, maggot filled words but by teaching them
how to read and count and love themselves more than they
love the lie of Charlton Heston's white knight fallacy.

This is not a protest poem because [i]'m not willing to stop:
stop funding my oppressor's war chest because French fries,

cola, and tennis shoes are more valuable to the bank of my
soul than dignity,
stop looking at the backside of my woman
long enough to see the inside of her glory,
stop being afraid of the cloudy shadow of unemployment
and the burning brand of low-class status,
stop lying that living like the oppressor doesn't mean
justifying the bulldozing of another bronze body.
This is not a protest poem because [i] continue to be made a
mental paraplegic by the state department of education,
fleeced by the finances of Discover Card, malnourished by
Burger King, and suffocated into surrender by Amsouth Bank.

This is not a protest poem because love is not my cast-iron
crest— not that televisional falsehood of universal
nothingness where we win when whites can realize how white
Blacks can be as in Desdemona's qualitative affection for the
Black ram in his ability to pour himself into the box of a white
sheep.

Love is...

> not letting Fannie Lou die broke
> going to li'l league baseball games when you'd
>   rather   spend Saturday in a sleep induced
>   coma
> saying awake at the PTA meetings after spending
>   all day working the chain-gang shift
> buying a child's winter coat when you want that
>   new laser disc player
> breaking adult conversation to hear the summer
>   breeze of a child's arbitrary outbursts
> letting out the pants of your lover's too tight slacks
> no ulterior motive other than to grow flowers of
>   self-esteem in our hearts
> not dependent on what brain-dead mockingbirds do
>   or say 'cause you were once a brain-dead
>   mockingbird and someone loved your
>   backward flying butt too.
> not fleeting like a cheap $20.00 high, last season's
>   designer suit, or fifteen minutes of sexual

bliss
not being afraid to die broke
swimming through an ugly reality to be baptized
in a beautiful Truth
an action verb with limitless amounts of
conjugation

So this can't be no protest poem 'cause
we be not protesting the lack of love.
When will we protest ourselves for allowing
love to fade away like last year's hit record?
Can we boycott men who don't want
to be Sun's to their seeds?
Can we sit-in schools with no community curriculum?
Can we picket religions that don't feed the hungry?
Can we boycott preachers who deliver Pharaoh's message?
Can we sit-in parties that use our platform as fertilizer fuel
for their machine and use our bodies as target practice
to show how middle of the road they are?
Can we picket politicians who line their pockets with
Judas' gold?
Can we boycott lawyers whose hands are stained with the
blood of the Ayers case?

No, this ain't no protest poem because we are
too inebriated off the glass phallus of middle-class-ism.
This ain't no protest poem because all of the Protestants
have invested in Satan's mutual funds.
This ain't no protest poem because
the Age of Enlightenment made a deity of capitalism
as we continue to kneel at the altar of a bull market.
This ain't no protest poem because [i] ain't willing to
"Hannibal Barca" you in the name of Black babies.
This ain't no protest poem because [i] ain't willing to
"Denmark Vesey" you in the name of Black liberation.
This ain't no protest poem because [i] ain't willing to
"Nat Turner" you in the name of Black women.
This ain't no protest poem because [i] ain't willing to
Toussaint L'Ouverture" you in the name of Black love.
This ain't no protest poem because
[i] continue to vote for oatmeal politicians

who have memorized King's speeches
while they vomit on his principles.
This is not a protest poem because [i] allow the 60s to be
prostituted by pulpit pimps and pyramid scam revolutionaries.

This is not a protest poem because
revolution begins with the fertile foundation of family.
Families are the atoms in society's molecular structure.
Families are the single cell organism
of the community's ecosystem.
Families are the mustard seed of the national oak tree.
Twenty years of integration, capitalism, and crack
weigh heavier on our families than the steel tonnage
of four hundred years of slavery.
Our families sit like abandoned houses
on dead-end streets pillaged and plundered
by smoked out transients and blind mice leaders.
Our families linger like decimated neighborhoods
filled with dysfunctional neighbors.
Our families give us as much chance as an
illiterate man in a speed reading contest.

This is not a protest poem because the clay of
family-hood has not been restructured.
When we celebrate families,
we mass-protest our destruction.
When we build families,
we demolish the straw hut of self-hate.
When we nurture families,
we provide kernels of nationhood.
When we fix the foundation of families,
we build a mighty army for Kujichagulia.
This is not a protest poem because
had this been a protest poem
we would all be filled with the swelling resolve
to find the buried treasure of love and
plant it into the soil of our families.

Writing Alone at Night
(for Li Po and Tu Fu)

The night pours my mind
like sweet sun kisses arouse
a flower's petals.

What's My Name?

My name is a wrought-iron trope dressed in a
W. E. B. Easter Suit with a J. C. Penny tie.
My name is not C Liegh McInnis.
My name is not Claude Lee McInnis, Jr.
My name is not CJ.
My name is not Claude.
My name is Li'l Claude,
son of Claudette who had a mirrored reflection named
Claude as she attended Walter Payton's alma mater and
met and married a man named Claude who was dubbed the
second coming, once removed[1], of Claude,
so what in the name of fallin' fruit from the tree
could I be but Li'l Claude,
Grandson of Ms. Rosalie Winfield who paid for her house
by collecting back interest owed on slavery by working
the be there all damn day shift at the New Roxy Theatre
on Issaquena Street in downtown Clarksdale, MS,
home and soil of root music known to most as the blues,
which was consummated at the crossroads
where every third quarter to come through the box office
went to Rosalie—which she used to pay for the home
where [i] was denominated and developed.

Names are more than labels, and having more than one
name chronicles the ebb and flow of a person —
like falling from African, to slave, to nigger, then climbing
to colored, to Negro, to Black, to African American, and
finally back to the crystal pure of African.
Names tell who you are, where you've been,
and where you're going.
Names even get at the budding potential of man,
like a mama naming her li'l man Prince or King or Warrior
in some scared Swahili tongue
or her li'l woman Queen or Gift from God.
Names even tell our misguided desires of where we'd like
to be like a sister naming her baby Mercedes or Porsche
or Cadillac even though they try to pronounce it Kadealick.

Names can be mirrors and foreshadows.
They can carry the lineage of a sacred antiquity
or they can carry the baggage of a stolen legacy
or they can show the artistry of how a people
with nothing but memory refashioned a counter-culture
to be used as an umbrella under the toxic rain of
colonization.

So when you address me as C. Liegh,
you are addressing the small evolution of me.
You are addressing Li'l Claude—
            the son of Claude and Claudette
You are addressing Rosalie's and Ruthie Mae's grand-man.
You are addressing the 'lectric man,
the teacher man, the poetry man
the workingman, and Monica's man.

That's why like water to a duck [i] ignore you
when you refuse to call me by my chosen name
'cause you're a cracked record stuck on stupid
dealing with my past, and
[i]'m a butterfly bursting from a cocoon,
evolving into my destiny,
or when you trip about a brother using a symbol for a name
never realizing that maybe we don't have enough colors
in our language to paint the essences of all of us.
Language is just a trope, a slip-sliding arbitrary trope, but a
trope nonetheless; so call me what you will;
but, you will call me as long as [i] keep cracking you over
your cranium with the lefts and rights of my metaphors and
images that quickly crossover world cable culturalization
and speak to Mississippi sensibilities, being proud that my
hands can pick cotton and write poetry, forging ahead when
the keepers of the canon tell me to stop.
You will call my name
in the middle of the night when the visions of my words
slip into your head's video game,
and [i] got you smelling the syrupy sugary smell of sugar
cane and swinging mountainous magnolia trees

on a spring breeze or the rotten fish funk of strange fruit
baptizing our memories in the name of tradition,
or you tasting the tart and bitter taste of the Truth
of pale teachers, ebony students, and senate bill 2239,
or you feeling a bone chilling breeze
that carries the weight of heavy rain and tornado season
like niggers standing on the verge of becoming Africans
or you hearing the lingering hollowed out calls of
Mississippi ghosts doomed to walk and work the face of the
Earth until Ole Miss justice gets 'round to laying their souls
to rest, or in my words you hear some faint, lingering cry of
Mississippi bards, rhapsodists, and troubadours
who, with their hands, sculpted the blueprint and
infrastructure of what is Mighty Merciless Magnolia
poetry, making me a
Black Boy like Richard Wright
or [i]'m Dr. Alexander's "Papa Chicken,"
or [i]'m singing *Belly Songs* like Etheridge Knight,
or becoming a Mississippi soothsayer like Jerry Ward
or Charlie Braxton's *Bluesman*
or being more Black than meets the eye
like David Williams,
or being a poet warrior like Jolivette Anderson.
But whatever [i] am and whatever [i] become,
[i]'m always willing to re-commune with my
Li'l Claude-ness

[i] have not been all things to all people,
but [i] have been many things to myself,
like all creatures of Earth constantly striving
to evolve to be the best me [i] can be.
And even when [i] have been other people at other times,
[i] remained me in all of my infinite me-ness.
On this rock [i] build my church:
the church of me
the institution of me
the religion of me
the philosophy of me
all of which are amalgamations of antecedent lives—

a moving, living history that is as old as man
making me the son of man, making me a man,
an Enos, an Adamite, a God, and a creator.

[i] am the original cockroach.
[i] was the singular cell spiritual seed
here before you, and [i]'ll be planted in this earth
after your swine-self has gorged all the grass and gone.
So, no matter how white-hot wretched and
Reaganomics raggedy you leave the planet,
my excrement and your decaying remains
will cultivate a flowerbed
helping me to refashion another world
for a whole new generation of Li'l Claudes

[1]My father was named after his Uncle Claude

Whatever "It" Is that We Want

For all the "it" in the world,
it will only be here
if we manifest **it**.

The Apology: Blood on the Typewriter
(Written the last Night [i] Had a Gun in my House)

Many people will say that this is a suicide note, but it isn't. It's an apology. An apology for never being able to sculpt the clay matter of myself into the type of artistic tool that my people need to be written into first-class citizenship. The edges of my pen's point have been too dull to strike a blow for freedom—as [i] have only scribbled vague markings of an individualized atom, dangling aimlessly in Norton's space of subjective significance.

Whether or not any one particular Dark brother sees himself in a struggle for first-class citizenship against the umbrella of white supremacy and all of its perverted manifestations is a philosophical issue—a way of seeing how the artifact furniture of our existence fits into the world's living room. But if one takes up this position, one has but one self-respecting choice—to become a solider in that struggle, a pen for progress. There are other choices, but they are not self-respecting because a man who will sellout his people for the token crumbs of self-preservation isn't deserving of human respect. With that in mind, one who understands this struggle has the responsibility of honing himself to do battle.

Doing battle comes in many forms. That is—we all have specific talents in life. The question is how do we use our particular "God-given" talents in our struggle for revolution? My chosen tool was writing. My battle was finding a way to use my writing in a manner that would inform, incite, and galvanize my people into positive action. [i] didn't want my writing to work or act as self-promotion of how much intelligence [i] carry around in my front pocket. [i] wanted my art to be sperm on the eggs of my people's lives, birthing actions of liberation. The Black writer's work must be like metaphysical bread that manifests itself in the fruitful actions of its readers. The best example of this is Baldwin, but there are more. King's and X's speeches do this. We must stay away from literary masturbation—writing just to get our intellectual rocks off. Our work must be so well informed and so well crafted that the mere experience of

96

reading it causes people to become better. Black writing must be a balm to the sores of Black people's lives. Check the works of Stephen Henderson, Larry Neal, Hoyt Fuller, Barbara Christian, and countless others. It must order the world or, in the least, help a reader in ordering his world. In short, the job of the writer is to point shit out to the reader and give the shit meaning. As Aristotle asserted, things are not real until they have meaning. Senate Bill 2239 wasn't real to most folks, especially Black folks, until the Mississippi Education Workers Group gave it meaning—showed 'em how suffocating this piece of plantation legislation was. That's all critical thinking is. Being able to assess and analyze information in a manner that we are able to show its meaning. What does this artifact of life mean, and how does it make us better? This is critical thinking, and this is what lets us know that we "be" educated. An educated person is not someone who can memorize facts. An educated person is someone who has the ability to use, dare [i] say, manipulate facts (raw data, information, materials, and resources), in a manner that makes their world better? So, a child should not be taught Algebra in a vacuum, as in a dog and pony show—merely learning this math as a way to demonstrate his intelligence, as in doing tricks. The child should be taught how Algebra can be used to make his world better, i.e., Bob Moses' Algebra Project. Now with that in mind the question remains, "Are we educating Black children?" My answer is no because to truly educate Black children is to declare revolution on America and all its institutions. So one of the primary jobs of Black artists is to educate.

Part of this education has to do with what Walter B. Rideout called "linguistic liberation." See, Barbara Christian states that writing is one of the primary manners in which we make or remake the world that we want to see exist. Again, Aristotle asserts that the poet doesn't copy life, but complete it. Thus, we, artists, are the completers (creators) of life. The problem for the Dark babies is that somebody other than us has been completing our world, completing our reality, for us, giving us a perverted view of the world by giving us a perverted view of ourselves. Our aesthetic is all twisted and poisoned because we judge the symmetry and balance of our faces by the scale and measurements of somebody else's. The ruler (measuring stick) of our mind doesn't match the dimensions of our being. That's because we are using somebody' else's yard stick. We must re-work this equation, and language is the best place to begin because language is the best container for a cold cup of Truth.

Language is the primary manner by which we transform the metaphysical into the physical—make ideas become words and words become concepts and concepts become actions and actions become movements. Think about it; the only thing that God ever made by hand was the body/shell of man. Everything else was "spoken" into being. So, we engage in creation through linguistic liberation when we take a language designed to oppress us and re-contextualize that language to meet our needs. This is a two fold action. The first step is to master the language. You can't re-contextualize that of which you don't have clear understanding. This means understanding the words and structure of language and understanding how language fits your needs. The second step, then, is to reshape or modify this language in a manner that fits your need. Richard Wright asserted that "If Black writers turned to their own vernacular traditions, Black literature could be as original and as compelling as Black music and folklore." The best example of this is the word "Black." African Americans simply decided to take this word from white folks. We refused to allow "Black" to have a negative connotation. The same must be done with our historical figures, such as Nat Turner, and with any fictional characters we create. There is no way that Columbus can be a heroic figure and Tuner not be heroic. Columbus murdered for exploitation and colonialism; Turner committed self-defense. We, as artists, must tell our stories. The flip side of this is that we must challenge our own people, especially with the images that we create of ourselves. It does not do any good to keep the oppressor from perpetuating negative stereotypes of us if we keep perpetuating them. (BET are you listening?) What we want is a wider variety of images. It's not that we have a problem with what is on television, radio, the big screen, and in Black books printed by white publishers. The problem is what is not on television, radio, the big screen, and in Black books printed by white publishers. There is no balance or holistic picture of African Americans in American media. Humanity is about balance. We, the artists, must demand balance. African people are the spectrum of humanity, yet our humanity is lost when we do not show the entire spectrum. But, if Truth be told, this balance will only come when we see ourselves as balanced. Most folks thought that this balance and humanity would come when we controlled (owned) something, but Bob Johnson proved that to be wrong. There is no balance at BET. There is no balance at BET because Johnson is a capitalist and not a humanitarian or a revolutionary. Johnson merely worked to prove Zora Neale Hurston's point that everyone who is my skin-folk ain't my kinfolk. Yet, rather than waste time persecuting Johnson, [i] need to spend time building a world. Johnson is but one man in a world of millions of Black people who are just as creative as he. It is not his fault that we wait for a messiah instead of moving our own mountains. The masses must liberate ourselves, and it begins with language so that we can become critical thinkers.

Why must we, at this time, master English?—because, at this time, it is the language of power. There is no other reason for Dark children to master English. Yet in mastering so called "English," we must force Americans to understand that no so-called American, even those beings who were merely appendages of Europe, has ever spoken English. There will never be a true American citizen until we acknowledge the American language. This means acknowledging the direct relation and contribution of African languages to the development of American language. This means acknowledging the contribution of Africa to the development of American civilization as well as acknowledging the contribution of Africa to the development of world civilization, which is what Du Bois is teaching in *The World and Africa*. Thus, humanity begins with language. It is the box in which we carry our humanity. With that understood, we must master it (English/American) and then use it for our benefit. It is the only language, tool, we have. Thus, poor writing is unacceptable. Weak imagery, worn metaphors, and unsubstantiated assertions are unacceptable in our battle. Not unacceptable because we are trying to impress white folks, but unacceptable because our people are so brainwashed that, in everything we do, we must prove to our own that we are worthy of their respect and trust by proving to be equal to white folks. This "normative white gaze," as Cornell West calls it, exists, and the only way that we are going to win this battle is to embrace it as one of our hurdles. The Black mind is impregnated and paralyzed by the "normative white gaze," and it is the job of the Black artist to abort the seeds of white supremacy and shake the Black nation from its paralysis. The Black writer has a duty to create a literature so powerful that we shake ourselves free from the emotional and psychological enslavement of the "normative white gaze." So we must, in our literature, show our own people how beautiful we are. Often that means showing how we, like very few others, have created beauty from nothingness—have created beauty from circumstances that would have and have killed other peoples. The Truth is that Greek, Roman, British, and white American culture exist on the backs and from the theft of other cultures. African and African American culture exist purely on the genius of its people, especially in their ability to fashion a culture when their culture has been taken by force from them. Additionally, the mastering of language includes, as Kalamu ya Salaam teaches, our need to master technology so we can do real battle with both CBS and BET. It does no good for the Black artist to have work for his people and no means to communicate that work to them.

My failure has been my inability to master language in such a manner that [i] move my people to action. My failure has been my inability to master language in such a manner that people who read my work want to be better people. My failure has been my inability to master language in such a manner that people who read my work want revolution, in all of its manifestations, today—right damn now! Because of this, [i] must silence the squeaky wheel of myself so that my people's liberation flows more smoothly. Yet before [i] take my leave, [i] must apologize to some people.

My literary mentors: Jolivette Anderson, David Brian

Williams, Marcus Uganda White, Ken Stiggers, Dr. Jerry W. Ward, Ahmos Zu-Bolton, Dr. Reginald Martin, Kalamu ya Salaam, Nayo Watkins, and Charlie Braxton.

My socio-political mentors: Big Mac, Sr., Dr. Ivory Phillips, Derrick Johnson, Hollis Watkins, Dr. Marie O'Banner Jackson, Attorney Alvin Chambliss.

Friends along the way—Ezra B., Brother Lukata, Johnny and Preselfannie, Angela R., Kurte P., Reagan "Black Steel," Nikki B., Howard R., Wanda M., M.U.G.A.B.E.E., Sherri W., Tufara, and Tony M.

Marcus Garvey stated that in order to grow or evolve, we must place ourselves amongst people who can nurture and inspire our growth or evolution. The above mentioned people have done that for me.

Jolivette you took me from being a computer poet to becoming a people's poet. You and David have taken poetry where it needs to be—where people live. You two, of course, were not the first, but you struggle, like so many, to continue the legacy of poetry as a people's art-form. You are a poet warrior, waging war on ignorance and hate.

David, you be good peoples. Your work reflects your family. In the vein of Zora Neale Hurston, you are not tragically colored but work to show that every river of color flows from the ocean of Blackness.

Ken, your mind is a treasure that [i] hope more will discover. By making us laugh at ourselves, we realize how stupid and silly we are, which allows us to change. As long as we can change, there is hope.

Dr. Jerry W. Ward, you've never given me bad advise. But more than anything, you've given me integrity. [i] know from where Charlie gets his integrity, and Charlie has more integrity than most people [i] know. Your unyielding and undying desire to promote Black humanity through the promotion of Black literature has been a deep river for me.

The Europeans were able to justify the enslavement of Black bodies by stripping them of their humanity. This was done by stripping them of their history. This was done by denying their legacy of literature. As James Weldon Johnson asserted, "The final measure of the greatness of all peoples is the amount and standard of the literature and art they have produced. The world does not know that a people is great until that people produces great literature and art. No people that has produced great literature and art has ever been looked upon by the world as distinctly inferior." Doc, you have fought to ensure that white people have not the ability to lie that they don't know about our legacy, and you have fought to ensure that Black writers hold to this flame so that their body of work does not become cold and barren from staying too long in the freezer of Eurodemia. But more importantly, you have fought to make sure that we, the Dark brothers, know of our humanity by knowing of our legacy of words that carries and cradles our humanity.

Charlie, you taught me that a writer ain't worth rotten paper if his word does not impregnate his people with knowledge and hope. As Baldwin asserted, writing is about getting at the Truth. If this is so, then a writer must be truthful with himself and his community. You have continued to do this, regardless of whether or not it hurt or hindered your publishing. Most importantly, by not feeding the people junk-food, people who know your work look to you for guidance and leadership. That's what being a writer is about.

Marcus, you taught me how to shut up. Poets "be" writing them long ass poems that call to mind James Brown's sentiments. They're "like a dull knife that jus' ain't cuttin', talkin' loud and sayin' nuthin'." You, on the other hand, make a haiku look lengthy. Besides that, you are true to your voice. Whenever [i] read you, [i] feel the muggy Mississippi night air and hear faint sounds of cafés and juke joints and Black folks singin' and cryin' and laughin' and ballin' and all that. Kalamu asserts that for a writer to be worth something he must be comfortable with the skin that he's in. That fits you. Man, you be wearing yo' skin like an old suit that never goes out of style. This allows your words to strike the bull's eye of our hearts and minds with Ginsu precision.

Father Zu, man you fed me food and wisdom, whether in your Flood Street crib, or in a New Orleans do-drop-in side street, back-alley eatery, or in your writer-in-residence loft. Missouri done messed around and let a brother with some bite get a position in the house. You be the Governor of Oliver Street. You be the roots in "The Family Tree." You be old man river with a muddy Black bottom in which Black folks need to take refuge to hide from the bottom feeders of injustice, picking away at our souls. Memory is a stainless steel sledgehammer, and the poet's job is to hit us over the head with that memory. [i] can't tell you how many headaches you have given me, forcing me to stay the course by forcing me to revisit my past.

Kalamu, you be a HBCU. You need to set up shop and charge tuition. Sometimes [i] wanna take all of your work, divided it into dime bags, roll it in some top papers, and transcend. You, like Jerry and Ahmos, give me integrity. [i] wanna be a "Cosmic Deputy." You taught me to be responsible for every word that [i] use and that life ain't nuthin' without theory to guide me. Thank you for being a funky drummer and showing us all where middle "C" is. P.S., you have done more than your share to make the world safe for love. All the children you've made and touched are your greatest poems.

Doc Martin, it ain't much like good food and good friends—is it? How much *Purple Rain* did we drink to see the *Sign "O" the Times*? Of course, *Everybody Knows What Time It Is*, but very few of us want to set the clock before it's too late. America's *Southern Secrets* keep rattling in our ear like the squeaky chair of Truth, calling us to respond, but our *Dysfunction Junction* causes us to continue on our merry inebriated way. With your work, you tried to get us to dance the "Dance Electric," but our iron souls are now too rhythm-less. Thank you for affirming that good literature needs to be funky, which means that we must be willing to step into some shit.

103

Nayo, one weekend with you got me off my ass and into work. Today is a day for work. We will rest when the Master calls us home. You be working our minds like sharecroppers worked the field. Thank you for teaching the world the beauty of every single butterfly. Each spirit, each soul, each body, and each person brings something to the parade. You have worked to remove the film of capitalism from our eyes so that we can see the eclectic colors of God more clearly.

All of y'all taught me to use my Black bullets to shoot white supremacy in the head.

Derrick, [i]'ve watched you fight against and for laws in the State Capitol, in schools, on back roads, and in election halls. [i]'ve seen you stare down icy cold blue eyes laced with serpentine retinas. [i]'ve driven darkened Mississippi back roads where we could hear the lingering ghosts of unresolved injustices. Of all the socially/politically relevant things that [i] have seen you do, the must poignant of these has been watching you raise your children. The Black revolution must begin in the home. In the same manner that the Black writer must be at war with the literary and linguistic stereotype, you were at war with the cultural stereotype. The same goes for my cousin George Fisher. No matter how many computers he's able to fix or program for Lucent labs, his greatest contribution to this Earth and to our evolution has been to raise his children well.

Hollis, thank you for talking to young folks when very few would. Thank you for tying a knot in the present to connect the past with the future.

Dr. Jackson, you taught me that ethics is politics. Thank you for loving your Dark self. Thank you for loving your Dark culture. Thank you for sharing all of that with me. My wife loves you because she knows that you helped her to keep me sane—well as close to it as you two could. Thank you for allowing me to rest my often times weary head on the bosom of your history.

The workers at Southern Echo, Echo is a family. Y'all taught me that you can't choose your family just like you can't choose the people in the struggle. We must find a way to work with those who want to work, not be too disappointed by those who don't want to work, develop the wisdom to know the difference, and also to get Hollis, Mike, and Leroy to always pay for lunch...Most importantly, thank y'all for feeding Mississippi's hungry with the nourishment of revolution.

Ezra you put your money where your mouth and heart are when it comes to creating art that makes Black people better. The baddest saxophonist [i] know, but even that pales to the work you do to open your crib to our community so that we can have a place to commune. Every arts movement had a center. Thanks for making your home our center.

Brother Lukata (Alvin Clark) you are a river that continues to flow and a tree that continues to grow. You have resuscitated and nurtured our Kwanzaa so that it could raise us from the dead.

The JSU and Jackson Heart Study students gave me life and energy every time [i] walked into a classroom.

To everybody on this list, [i] loved to hear y'all talk to white folks with the same trumpeted tone that they talk to us. Besides my father, Hal Dockins, you were one of the first Black men [i] saw do this. You've shown me that mentorship is not about going to a depraved place. Mentorship is showing a child an alternative to that depravation. Man, [i] didn't have a clue before [i] started working for you. [i] had some theory, some concepts of how [i] thought the world did and should work. You gave me the opportunity to put that theory into practice and let me learn that [i] didn't know shit, but that was alright 'cause you were going to let me learn, no matter how many times [i] fucked up.

John, the big dog, the biggest dog of 'em all, keep barking until people hear the message; we are on this Earth to love each other and enjoy good music & food. Thank you for giving the world your pure spirit.

G. Fish: A father on the floor with his two children—crayons, pillows, and peanut butter and jelly. Your live is a beautiful poem.

Rikki G. and Morris. We gets funked up on the one. Welcome to the Dawn, Cousins. We be using purple poetry to ease *Chaos and Disorder*, knowing that only love will Emancipate us. It's "Thunder" as long as we know that the only love there is is the love we make. Peace and be wild.

Pops—what is a man? You taught me to keep asking this question and to keep searching for many answers. Your light has proven that manhood is being what women need us to be when they need us to be it. X and Y. Ying and Yang. Adam and Eve. We are here to complete each other, not control each other. Thanks.

Mother. Love is, isn't it? You have been love to me. When you had nothing else, you gave love to me. [i] know that love is all that one can give. It's all that we should want.

To Monica (Soul of my Soul). Don't think that this is anything that you have done wrong. You loved me best you could. Most days, you were the only reason [i] woke up. Often, [i] hated going to sleep for fear of never seeing you again. You make me better. The only word [i] have for you is peace—this is what you are to me and what you deserve in life. [i] don't know any tomorrows, but [i] know enough yesterdays to know that there is a heaven, and it flows through the glow in your eyes and the summer warmth of your smile. As [i] lay me down to sleep and pass over to the other side, it is your love that comforts me into being able to open doors with no walls.

Peace, rain, and sunshine...
rainbows forever,
C. Liegh McInnis,
Jackson, Mississippi, January 2001

106

www.ingramcontent.com/pod-product-compliance
Lightning Source LLC
Chambersburg PA
CBHW032144040426
42449CB00005B/390